MONTANA BACKROADS

By Beverly R. Magley

Montana Magazine
American & World Geographic Publishing
Helena, Montana

MONTANA
GEOGRAPHIC
SERIES

NUMBER 19

DEDICATION

For Ginny, Judy, Tim, and Ed, who shared thousands of miles of backroads with me and never once complained about stopping for the fiftieth time that morning. May our laughter still echo along the roads.

14·95 PB ✓

ACKNOWLEDGMENTS

I am grateful to the fine people around the state who opened their homes and lives to brighten the pages of this book; who illuminated that sense of place felt by every Montanan. With thanks to Rock Ringling, John Gatchell, Susan Bryan, and to many other friends for extending my contacts throughout the backroads communities of Montana.

Cataloging in Publication information

Magley, Beverly.
   Montana backroads / by Beverly R. Magley.
      p. : ; cm. -- (Montana geographic series ; no. 19)
   Includes index.
   ISBN 1-56037-033-5
      1. Montana--Guidebooks. 2. Montana--Description and travel--1981- 3. Automobile travel--Montana--Guidebooks.   I. Title.   II. Series.
F729.3.M33 1993
917.8604'33--dc20   93-16144

Above: *Golden hours.* PAUL VUCETICH
Facing page: *Sunset on Flathead Lake.* JOHN REDDY
Title page: *U.S. Highway 89, northwestern Montana.* DOUG DYE
Front cover: *Along the Rocky Mountain Front near Heart Butte.* JOHN REDDY
Back cover: *Rainbow near Wilsall.* WAYNE MUMFORD

Text © 1993 Beverly R. Magley
© 1993 American & World Geographic Publishing
All rights reserved.

Printed in Hong Kong.

CONTENTS

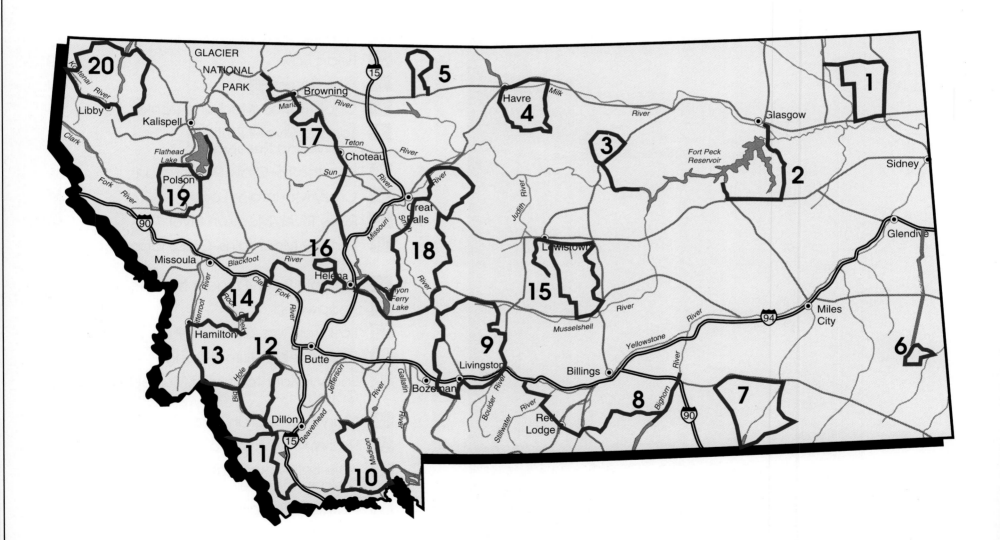

INTRODUCTION

Montana infiltrates your being just as surely as the smell of cooking popcorn permeates a home. Some places fill your senses; Montana fills your soul.

The most interesting thing about backroads travel is that you're not going anywhere. There's no hurry. It's not destination-oriented. Be right where you are at the moment, and stop for whatever catches your fancy.

Traveling Montana's backroads is about conversations with locals, about swapping stories, about delays and detours and slow-paced movement. About pulling over for a herd of cows and calves; forking over a donation for the volunteer fire department at the sidewalk bake sale; finding out you've arrived just in time for the county rodeo.

Acquire a traveling portfolio of Forest Service and BLM maps. Forget the state highway map—a lot of these roads aren't even on it. Some of the roads are closed by snow each winter. Take a compass, a map, water, and munchies. Don't expect any of the little towns to have gas, food, or even a telephone. If there is a gas station, it's probably not open on weekends or evenings. And to get a tankful of gas on a weekday, you may have to go find the station owner at the local cafe.

Ask the locals if a road is passable, and take their advice. Be willing to draft Alternate Route B or C on the spur of the moment. Don't drive the dirt roads when they're wet. Don't even consider it.

The condition of unpaved roads varies by the day. If it has been dry and the county road-graders were active, the routes are a delight. If the road crew has been elsewhere, or a thunder-boomer dumped its load of moisture recently, the roads can develop a slippery topography that's either not passable, or is simply no fun.

Ask questions. Ask the people who live there. They know. And if they don't know, they know who does. Get hooked on the slower pace of travel, of rarely exceeding 25 miles per hour, of finding a wonderful place and just by God staying there for a while.

Enhance your travel with a magnifying glass, binoculars, journal, camera, and field guides to birds and flowers and trees. Stop when something catches your eye. I watched a roadside wheat harvest and ended up aboard the combine; puzzled out how they hay with a beaverslide and found myself riding the hayrake; took pictures of a lovely cabin and was invited in for lunch.

There's a price to pay for compulsive backroads travel: I replaced shocks, struts, tires, windshields, and even the engine mount. You may have to adjust to "regular" travel occasionally, when driving the interstate feels like hurtling through space aboard the Challenger.

Stop. Look closely around you then far away; listen to the night sounds and the morning songs; smell the crops, dry fields, and moist riverbanks. Change your plans on the spot. Bring some good instrumental music. Solo flute, classical guitar, jazz piano. Play music that has a rhythm and cadence that enhances the rise and fall of the land, with instruments that blend with the murmur of rivers and melody of songbirds.

Stop and talk. Montanans are here because we love it—after all, it would be easier to live in a balmier clime—so right away Montanans have something in common. Listen to people refer to the sense of place found here. The description may sound different from a rancher or a state worker; different from a teacher or a miner. But each touches on that sense of place, of knowing that there's enough room here, of belonging.

Perceive the wildness still tangible, still paramount, in this sense of place, this place Montana.

ROB OUTLAW

Gravel road through farm near Wilsall.

1 High Plains

Northeast Montana is not at the ends of the earth. Nor is it truly flat like the unwavering plains of Nebraska, Kansas, and eastern Colorado.

Northeast Montana is a land of gentle swales and dips and shallow coulees; low badlands and prairie potholes and tiny creeks; wheatfields and oil derricks and prairie grasses. It's a place to appreciate subtle contours and expansive spaces. You need a wide-angle lens to do justice to this country.

Northeast Montana is big country and small towns. A fine combination.

In Culbertson, a youngster led his very fat, very shiny, black pony down the street. Both were decked out in full cowboy regalia. Vehicles jammed with people drove by, scrubbed faces shining below the brims of cowboy hats. Five passengers waved American flags from the back of a pickup. All were headed for the Culbertson Pony Club rodeo arena.

There are very few bleachers at the rodeo arena. But there was little need for bleachers. Most of the audience sat in their vehicles on the hill by the arena, watching through the windshields. Since handclapping doesn't carry well through automobile glass, they leaned on the horns to show approval for a good ride.

I watched from the bleachers, highly entertained by the events and by the "backstage" goings-on. Along with the every-day sort of rodeo events, Culbertson rodeoers compete in North Dakota Surfing, where horses gallop full speed, each dragging a clown trying frantically to balance on a board.

A light haze of dust permeated the entire arena, providing a translucent quality that needed only slow-motion action to make it dream-like. However, the thuds and grunts from contestants hitting the ground were decidedly undreamlike.

Gene Foss was running the arena gate. He took his job seriously, but found plenty of moments to explain why Culbertson is such a fine place to call home. Every summer there are assorted community activities: Missouri River Poker Float,

Pioneer Days and Rodeo, a wooden-wheel-only Covered Wagon Train trek complete with evening dance, a Threshing Bee, and the Roosevelt County Fair. He spoke of the 187 entries in the rodeo parade just that morning, the largest parade he could remember.

Is he a rodeo competitor? "Naw. I'm a bit stiff yet from branding," he said, smiling. "We did quite a few. Well, we've got our own, and the neighbors helped us. So we got to go help them, and so on, till it was about six thousand done. So rodeoin' doesn't look so inviting right now."

The street dance after the rodeo was an interesting snippet of rural America. A slew of teenagers clustered on the corner and watched each other watch each other standing there. A few moms danced with their kids. Intermittently, trains thundered by a block away, drowning out the band. Trying to get into the Montana Bar was like trying to get into a Butte bar on St. Patrick's Day—no chance. A nine-year-old tried to teach her four-year-old brother some dance steps, to no avail. They abandoned the effort and just enjoyed wriggling and bouncing to the beat. One teenage couple braved the many eyes and two-stepped a few dances.

We left and drove north, stopping for the night in Froid. Two very enthusiastic boys bicycled ahead to show us where to camp in the city park. This is what people mean when they talk about small town advantages—these communities welcome travelers by providing free campsites, and their youngsters can safely burn off energy on a summer night by bicycling around town at midnight.

We awoke to mourning doves calling from the grain elevators, and set breakfast on the picnic table, to find we'd

Above: Barrel racing is a highly competitive event for women rodeo contestants.

Facing page: Hoarfrost's geometric platelets cling to winter vegetation.
MICHAEL CRUMMETT

After a good rainfall, northeastern Montana can look like the Emerald City.

BRUCE SELYEM

camped right across the caragana hedge from my Helena neighbor. Throughout my travels in out-of-the-way places, I have run into people I know. At that moment, we were all nearly 500 miles from home. We really do live in a small town called Montana.

North of Froid, Medicine Lake is a startling sight in the prairie landscape. The surrounding wilderness and national wildlife refuge provide over 31,000 acres of lake, wetlands, and mixed-grass prairie habitats. It's a rare opportunity to see native grasslands that never have been tilled under. Avid bird-watchers, lists in hand, are in paradise here identifying songbirds like McCown's longspurs or Sprague's pipits.

Casual observers like me have a front-row seat on enough wildlife activity to keep anyone interested. In spring up to 30,000 ducklings and 800 goslings bob around on the lake. White pelicans congregate to raise more than 2,000 young every year. Hormone-saturated sharp-tailed grouse drum themselves into exhaustion on the leks, trying to attract the nonchalant females. White-tailed deer browse around old bison bones and tipi rings.

Northeastern Montana was the last part of Montana settled by whites. There is a rich, and very accessible, history here. Hunkpapa Sioux Chief Sitting Bull followed Big Muddy Creek to make his surrender at Fort Buford. Later, Butch Cassidy and assorted other outlaws, rustlers, and bootleggers hid in the labyrinth of gulches along that same creek. Plentywood-area farmers organized a Communist movement in the 1920s.

Sheridan County residents obviously hold the past in high regard. The Sheridan County Museum in Plentywood is stuffed with historic articles within its lichen-covered rock walls. Outside, the Agriculture Museum displays a wonderful collection of tractors, threshers, combines, plows, and wagons. Walk around these well-kept machines and imagine some early farmer's excitement at acquiring the newest and best implement. It's rather mind-boggling to see a bucket of firewood attached to a tractor, located so the driver could easily feed the wood-burning engine.

Pioneer Town in Scobey is another admirable museum. But Scobey is an admirable community. Just 1,154 people live here. Judging by the projects and clubs and celebrations, at least 1,000 of them must be community activists, or else a fair number of "wanna-be" Scobeyites come for a lot of extended visits.

Scobey's 35-piece Prairie Symphonette was featured on television on "Portrait of America." This unique local orchestra is likely to have retired grandparents playing violins next to a cello-stroking farmer next to flute-tooting cousins next to drum-playing grandchildren. Those wanting to play different styles of music can be found in the local Dixieland Jazz Band or Big Band.

Local history is very interesting. The community hired baseball's blacklisted Chicago Blacksox to help Scobey beat Plentywood in the 1920s, and it houses the county courthouse in a former brothel (yes—it's still in that same building). Four Buttes west of town was once known as Whiskey Buttes because early traders rendezvoused here to exchange whiskey for furs.

After weeks on the road I was thoroughly saturated with typical rural restaurant-fried everything. Shu's Kitchen on 1st Avenue was a welcome find. Shu hails from Thailand but married a local Scobey boy. The simple cafe surroundings didn't prepare me for her excellent Oriental cuisine. Yum!

Alvin and Dorothy Rustebaake farm just west of Scobey. We dropped in one Sunday afternoon, when several daughters and about seven of their 21 grandchildren were zooming around the yard. "You never quite know who will show up on a Sunday," Dorothy laughed. "It keeps us guessing."

Dorothy is a writer, and publishes short stories, poems, children's stories, and magazine and newspaper articles. The Rustebaakes' home is full of family photos and books. It's easy to imagine Dorothy on a wintery morning, telling stories and flipping pancakes on the giant coal-burning cook stove.

The Rustebaakes are not your typical dryland wheat farmers. In 1975 Alvin was out in his wheatfields spraying for pests, and suddenly questioned why he was putting poison on food. "I put the sprayer away and never used chemicals again," he said. "It's one of the best decisions I've ever made." The Rustebaakes now grow organically-certified grains.

"I used to take my whole harvest into town, get paid, and go to the bank and make payments," Alvin said. "Then I'd borrow money to buy groceries on the way home. Organic farming got us out of that cycle."

The Rustebaakes opened their Great Grains Milling Company in 1979. They grind only organically grown wheat, and sell it in Montana, North Dakota, South Dakota, and Wyoming. Great Grains products are well-respected and the company's recipes are featured in several cookbooks. One hundred twenty pounds of their pancake and waffle mixes were gobbled up at the thresherman's breakfast during Scobey's last Pioneer Days.

Alvin showed me through the mill, enthusiastically explaining about the bolter, hoppers, sieves, spouts, and so on. His mill grinds about 300 pounds of flour an hour, and he bags the flour himself. He makes stone-ground whole wheat and golden wheat flour; rye, barley, and pasta flours; cracked wheat cereal; bran; and pancake and waffle mixes.

"My son John is a mechanical whiz," he exclaimed. "They wanted ten thousand dollars for a new mixer for our pancakes, and he made one for almost nothing. He used an old washing machine motor, a barrel, and rollers from a clothes dryer, and welded a frame. The only thing we bought were some pulleys."

South of Scobey and Flaxville, this backroads route trundles across the Fort Peck Indian Reservation. The land has few

Throughout my travels in out-of-the-way places, I have run into people I know. At that moment we were all nearly 500 miles from home. We really do live in a small town called Montana.

Above: *A robin finds a sheltered nesting site in the farm implements at Sheridan County's Agriculture Museum.*

Facing page, clockwise from left: *White pelicans cruise the waters at Medicine Lake National Wildlife Refuge. The meadowlark, Montana's state bird. Farmers cultivate grain right up to the edge of cliffs and badlands in eastern Montana.*

undulations and could conceivably be labeled flat. Yet even here, you may top a rise and see the Missouri River Breaks thirty miles distant, or look east over the meanderings of the Poplar River.

Poplar sits at the confluence of the Poplar and Missouri rivers. Amtrak parallels Highway 2 along the riverbanks. Westbound passengers, bored from staring at the preceding miles of unvarying prairie, perk up and lose their stupefied gazes. Here the route reveals intriguing gulches and hidden niches; lush green riverbanks and islands; badlands of eroded hoodoos and spires.

Pat Beck grew up in Poplar, left, then returned for good. "You get bonded to the land and the people," she said. "My father homesteaded here. This is home."

Beck spearheaded the centennial publication *Poplar Montana Almanac 1892-1992*. She said it was way too much work, but she glowed as brightly as her tie-dyed T-shirt when speaking of the project.

"I got coerced into doing it," she laughed. "I had in mind a centennial pamphlet." A year and a half and nearly 250 pages later, the almanac was finished.

"It became such a big thing in our lives," she said. "You get one story and then they say, 'Oh, you should talk to so-and-so,' and on it went. Some of the old-timers came into our store almost every day and told story after story. I miss them now."

Beck said there's another whole book's worth of stories that were too sensitive to publish. "It's amazing—there are a lot of families who still want to hide something that happened a hundred years ago."

"I ponder a lot of things, like the tunnels that connected the restaurant to the showhouse. I look at the town differently now. I think, 'Gee, the parade grounds were there fifty years ago.' Or my friends dig in their gardens and find relics and arrowheads. It's very tangible."

Beck cherishes the diversity within the community, and

said she loves the Indian celebrations. "I like to dance with the Indian people. There are no barriers then—they make you feel so welcome. I love the smell of wood smoke, and the feasting and giveaways. Drums go all night, with people singing and dancing and talking."

Poplar has many amenities not usually available to a town of 881 residents. The tribe has built a roller skating rink, tennis court, and swimming pool, as well as a school and hospital. "They never say, 'You go somewhere else—you're white'," Beck stated. "Somewhere the roles have changed and they're so gracious about sharing with us."

Beck's face saddened as she spoke of changes and economic struggles in the community. "If you live here long enough, you feel like all-family. If somebody's not well, we're all sad. When someone dies we all feel the loss."

Beck's strong connection to Poplar is evident in the introduction to the almanac, where she wrote "...there is an invisible bond between the people and this land...they have heard the whispered music in the grass, seen the purple crocus grow in spring, and smelled the pungent sage as they have passed..."

Steve Gray Hawk is the captain of the police force in Poplar. "In the Army they called me Chief instead of Sarge," he recalled. "When I got this job I said I wanted to be a captain, not a chief."

Gray Hawk is proud to live and work in his hometown, but he mourns the rapid loss of the old culture. "When I was young, all old people were respected and called grandmother and grandfather. They were our teachers as we went into the world."

He remembers wearing government-issued clothing and hobnail shoes. "When we went to school all the little Indian kids had to take off their shoes and line them up at the door so we wouldn't ruin the floor. Clothing came in bundles, by size.

We wore army coats with gold buttons, and got in trouble if we 'spoke Indian.' Now they're trying to teach it and bring it back."

Gray Hawk is extremely proud of the tribally owned and operated A & S Tribal Industries and Multiplex West. "Those people work so hard, and are determined to make it succeed. If the government programs would step out and let us make a living like we should, the rest of my people would be okay too. How can you be expected to work to get ahead if you're offered something for nothing?"

He believes that alcohol and drugs have a stranglehold on his people, and sees prejudice getting worse, not better. "Not in Poplar, though," he added. "Here there are lots of intermixed marriages. In Poplar you know everybody and can depend on people. We work together as family."

2 Fort Peck Country

Highway 200 through Jordan is one of the least-traveled paved highways in Montana. Hell Creek Recreation Area lies 25 graveled miles north of Jordan. Don't worry about the "maddening crowd" here.

This is the Big Open, the Big Dry. It might also be called the Big Friendly—if you can find a person, it's a cinch that he or she'll be glad to chat.

Jordan is the most isolated county seat in the contiguous United States. The county dormitory houses high-school students who live too far away to commute every day. It's the last dorm of its kind in Montana.

Ranching is the community's mainstay. Each cow forages on about 25 acres of land—and there are no obese bovines in sight. Abandoned homesteaders' shanties now shade those cows, or they house chickens or farm equipment.

Pyramidal buttes are scattered across the landscape like some child's neglected blocks. One of these seemingly nondescript buttes caused a considerable stir among geologists when the mineral armalcolite was identified there. Armalcolite had previously been found only in rocks collected on the moon.

A layer of ancient dust in that same butte contains stishovite (another rare mineral), and some distinctive fracture patterns. Stishovite and those fractures form only in mind-bogglingly massive explosions. These findings support the theory that 65 million years ago a gigantic meteorite struck the earth, and the resulting dust cloud contributed to the demise of the dinosaurs. Remains of some of those very dusty dinosaurs have been excavated in the badlands along the Missouri, to the north.

The road to Hell Creek Recreation Area descends through twelve miles of eroded, sculpted landforms to reach Fort Peck Reservoir. Rounded mounds, pointed towers, and flattened slabs are painted in striated colors that tell primeval stories of coral reefs, river deltas, deserts, and jungles.

The turquoise water in the reservoir is an obvious attraction here in the Big Dry. But when it's cool, walk through the sage up into the coulees of the C.M. Russell National Wildlife Refuge. There's a whole other world in those dry gulches.

Finding no wildlife to look over at a wildlife overlook, I filled the thermos and strolled off to other vantage points, small dust storms surrounding each step.

An unidentified rodent squeaked and scurried to the protection of a large sagebrush. A buzztail (rattlesnake) issued a warning not to come closer—I obliged willingly, and chose another route up a hill.

Occasionally there's time to sit, sipping tea, not really looking for anything. Isn't that when they say you see the most? My view slid rapidly from macrocosmic musings about badlands geology to a focused interest in the goings-on of a family (tribe? race?) of ants. These ants were traveling a well-worn ant highway, antennae waving vigorously. Ants' olfactory organs are on their antennae. They cooperate completely with members of their own colony, who all smell the same. But woe to a trespasser smelling like a different colony! Ant wars are every bit as brutal and heinous as human wars. Red ant victors even take black ant cocoons and raise the hatches as slaves.

Numerous alarms interrupted my reverie—ground squirrel whistles and magpie squawks—caused by a coyote trotting along the trail below, nose to the ground, quite oblivious to anyone's presence.

After finishing my tea, I stretched out to watch the sunset cloud show. This was a ringside seat—the colors eventually engulfed the entire western horizon and extended overhead in a wash of pastel tones.

East of Jordan the highway cuts an undeviating course through the rolling prairie. The clouds above mimic the contours of the buttes and badlands below. Sheep look like little splotches of alkaline salt in the dry fields.

The route runs through a miniature painted desert near Little Dry Creek, which lives up to its name most of the year.

Highway 24 runs north to Glasgow. The drive is a sort of "bear went over the mountain" experience. Each rise in the road promises to offer that all-encompassing view, until you top the rise and see yet another rise ahead. And again. And again.

But the near vista is intriguing. Potholes of water and reeds are enclosed by badlands and hills and coulees. Natural features are etched with sharp profiles. There is no gentleness to this landscape. Put on polarized sunglasses and drive either early or late in the day, when shadows add interesting hues.

About midway to Fort Peck, a lone phone booth stands by the side of the road. There is not a structure in sight—not even a ranch within view. Just one, lonely, telephone booth. Hmm.

I drove in blinding sunlight through miles of yellow sweet clover lining the roadside. The wind jostled the vehicle mercilessly, and cottonwood branches lunged back and forth in the draws. A spectacular storm arose off to the east: the tops of the clouds brightly lit with sunshine; the middle dark and dense; the cloud base a flat black brew throwing streamers of rain and bolts of lightning to the shadowed earth below.

Fort Peck Dam is one of those engineering marvels that mostly only engineers marvel about. Many of the rest of us see a big dirt slope with a road on top, next to a lake. To be sure, I can be amazed at the fact that the 130 million cubic yards of dirt and rocks comprising the dam would fill boxcars that, placed end to end, could encircle the globe at the equator. I'm impressed that the dam impounds waters draining more than 57,000 square miles. And, I have benefited from the recreation areas along the shores, and appreciate the wildlife refuge adjoining the reservoir.

Nevertheless, all dams leave me with a certain sense of sorrow and dread. Sorrow for the river's interrupted cycle of flood and ebb, for the tremendous evaporation of water in this arid country. Dread at the environmental damage we do when impounding vast quantities of silt-bearing waters.

What brings me joy is learning about the sense of community and pride felt by those who worked together to make this dam. Any project requiring such total cooperation for a common goal is a wonderful achievement, humanity at its best.

Fort Peck Dam was one of the nation's biggest New Deal work projects. Construction began in 1933. The dam and electric powerhouses were completed in the early 1940s, after the pumping of over $110 million into the state economy to harness Missouri floodwaters and generate electricity. It is the third largest earth-filled dam in the world and Montana's largest man-made alteration of the land.

Decades away from the hurtling bustle of boom town dam-building days, the town of Fort Peck is a pleasant community. A few structures remind you of those times: the Fort Peck Theatre, Fort Peck Hotel, and Big Shot Row—the stately homes that once housed the managers of the project.

As new owners of one of those houses, Brenda and Ted Shye were enthusiastically repairing cracked plaster, painting walls, adding storm windows and insulation, and generally making it habitable.

"I had a real twinge about buying this house," Brenda said. "It occurred to me that someone was living here in luxury, with servants and all the amenities, while my family was living in shanties or shacks down below. It was practically a castle back then."

Brenda's grandfather was one of many who lost their farms during the Depression. The dam project provided much-needed work for many of her relatives in this area. She grew up hearing her father and uncles tell about working on the dam. "There were some big disasters, like the slide, but they mostly talked about the good times," she said. "They were thrilled to have jobs. The theater ran twenty-four hours a day, and there were always get-togethers with other families."

It's a real adjustment for the Shyes to move into Fort

There is no gentleness to this landscape.

Put on polarized sunglasses and drive either early or late in the day, when shadows add interesting hues.

Top left: *Intriguing badlands surround much of Fort Peck Reservoir.*
Top right: *Beauty, solitude, and fishing at Fort Peck Reservoir.*

Facing page: *Spillway at Fort Peck Dam.*

Peck, where the trees and hills limit the view. They grow wheat on their Glasgow-area farm and on leased acreage north, south, east, and west of Fort Peck. Farming over such a wide area is almost a crop insurance, because in a given year one place might get hail, or another gets better rain.

"It makes sense to live here, right in the middle of our operations," Brenda stated. "But up on the fields you can see so far. It's that sense of being in an air traffic control tower. You can see if there's a fire in someone's haystack, or notice a storm coming hours before it hits, that kind of thing."

The Shyes stretch themselves beyond the family farm. "We got into politics so we can think about something besides the price of wheat and the rainfall," Brenda laughed.

Ted is a state legislator, and Brenda has lobbied for the Montana Women's Lobby, and worked on legislation concerning developmental disabilities programs and the Montana Cultural Advocacy. They both love the intellectual stimulation and cultural events in Helena, but are strongly tied to farming.

"I sometimes wish we had some more things here, like public radio and TV," Brenda said. "But you just have to focus on what you do have. This spring I had to look so hard for a wildflower that I was thrilled to find one. Maybe you get jaded in a place where things are easy and accessible.

"I remember a quote from a woman homesteader," she continued. "It went, 'Well, I had everything that I ever wanted. But I was never foolish enough to wish for something I knew I couldn't have.' You have to have that attitude to live here and be happy. Like anywhere."

3 Little Rockies/Missouri River

Nearly 100 degrees with no clouds in sight—a van with food, water, extra clothing, and emergency medical supplies rolled slowly east along the highway, warning lights flashing. In front, an Indian ran with sweat streaming down his trim torso. The prayer flags skittered around the baton he carried, while his arms pumped forward and back.

This runner would hand the prayer flags off to others taking part in the 14th annual "Sacred Run Turtle Island 1992." Volunteers run from Alaska south to New Mexico to meet their counterparts, who run from the southern tip of South America—Tierra del Fuego—north to New Mexico. They carry the message that all living things are sacred, and that we humans are related to all species of life. The Montana route took them through Rocky Boy's Reservation, Fort Belknap Reservation, and Fort Peck Reservation.

I watched the hand-off at Fort Belknap Agency. Runners were smudged with smoke from sweet pine, sage, cedar, and sweetgrass. Prayers were offered. My prayer joined theirs.

Viewed from the north, the Little Rocky Mountains are a wonderland of green, an Emerald City of wildlife, timber, and streams in the midst of the arid plains. Limestone cliffs wrap around the range like medieval walls enclosing a castle.

The Gros Ventre and Assiniboine tribes hold a Sun Dance in the shelter of Mouse Canyon. At summer camp in Mission Canyon, children can study the Gros Ventre or Assiniboine language and learn traditional beadwork, quilling, and hide tanning. Eagle Child Butte juts above the other peaks, a sacred site for traditional vision quests and a place to find health, peace, and good feelings.

Driving west around the Little Rockies, you'll see a number of interesting things. Old mission church buildings still stand, framed by the mountains. A major forest fire in 1988 burned the slopes; today abundant wildflowers and grasses are reclaiming the soil. My favorite sight here was the stark white of tipi and basketball hoop, backdropped by the charred timber on the hill.

South of the mountains, the view extends over rolling hills, across the Missouri Breaks and on south across the prairie. It's a vision of pastoral peacefulness.

But drive east around the Little Rockies. These mountains are besieged, and despite the barricading walls they are losing. A massive low-grade heap-leach gold mine produces about $10 million of gold and silver a year for a Washington-based corporation. Cyanide periodically pollutes the groundwater and local streams, killing wildlife. Dynamite and heavy equipment propel dust into the air. The fish in Peoples Creek are dead. Truckload by truckload, the mountains are being dismantled.

Today's spiritual seekers who climb Eagle Child Butte on a vision quest see, hear, and smell the mine. What revelations could Moses have experienced on Mount Sinai if such a mine had operated there?

Seventy-nine-year-old Dora Helgeson has ranched with her family on the north edge of the Little Rockies for 55 years. We sat in the shade of a box elder tree, admiring the hollyhocks. Her primary concern at that time was water quality being compromised by cyanide from Pegasus Gold Mine. "They're tearing apart our mountains," she said. "Now they're going to poison our water." She worries about her cattle, the fish, and the Juneberries and chokecherries that grow along the banks. "We have to fight to have clean water. That's not right."

Helgeson is one of about 40 people who still speaks Assiniboine. She is involved in the efforts to record the language before it's too late. "When I grew up they said to forget the Indian ways, be like white people," she said. "Now they say, 'Bring back your culture, your language. You're losing it.' But now is fifty years too late."

Helgeson said young people will be lucky to learn the basic words, like colors, numbers, days, and relationships. She chuckled when telling of an enthusiastic youngster who asked her how to say "pizza" in Assiniboine.

She sees improvements on the Fort Belknap Reservation, such as better housing and the community college, but feels that town bunches people together too much. "When you live on the land you take care of it," she said. "That's the best place to be, out here with the mountains and the grasslands. I'll stay right here until I die."

South of the Little Rockies, Highway 191 drops suddenly, constricting your long-ranging prairie view of the world into the intimacy of the Missouri River Breaks. A 20-mile self-guided auto tour begins just north of the bridge and loops east and north along the river and up to splendid views across the prairie, and then turns west again to meet the highway. Interpretive signs along the way explain the river and prairie ecosystems, geology, and history.

It's a fine loop, but it required leaving the river bottom sooner than I wanted to. Instead, I just kept driving along the river roads for about nine miles. The road curled alongside the bends in the river, climbed up around bluffs, and drifted through stands of ponderosa. Eastern kingbirds perched atop tall sagebrush, deer watched to see if they should be frightened, prairie-dog road warriors challenged themselves to run under the moving vehicle, anglers lazed along the riverbank.

It's a very slow route. A person needs to get out and fish, spread out a picnic, shoo the cows off the road, spread out a blanket and hope for a show of northern lights or shooting stars. Multiple side roads are inflicted on steep bluffs. It's a puzzle to figure out which fork in the road is most inviting. But just mosey along. The rattling in your brains will tell you when it's time to leave this washboard route.

I set camp on a bluff about 400 feet above the river, then took a brisk walk, swinging my arms and stepping out, stretch-ing, running full-tilt-boogie down the inclines to feel the long strides pull open my hip sockets and release the sitting-in-the-car lethargy.

The July night was balmy, with soft air. Smells of dusty dry badlands and pungent sage mixed with the night insects' clicks and rings. The world made an indiscernible transition from fading daylight to muted gibbous moonlight. A single pelican floated on the oxbow in the river.

Tranquillity. Then a brief flurry of coyote yips and yowls—a family reunited? Firing up to separate for the night's hunt?

A solid bank of clouds hung up on the Bears Paw Mountains to the west let loose one spectacular orange-red twisted bolt of lightning that was jagged like these myriad coulees. The Missouri River gleamed moonlight and I hearkened back to November canoe trips on this waterway: sunshine and wearing light sweaters some years; sub-zero and wear-everything-you-brought other years. Sometimes we chopped a hole in the riverbank ice just to launch the canoes; sometimes it was a mud-slog to land at a campsite. Travel is never commonplace on the Missouri River.

Montana blesses us with places that feed the spirit.

Eastern kingbirds perched atop tall sagebrush, deer watched to see if they should be frightened, prairie-dog road warriors challenged themselves to run under the moving vehicle, anglers lazed along the riverbank.

Right: *Missouri River Breaks.*

Facing page: *View east toward the Little Rockies from Mt. Baldy in the Bears Paws.*

A network of dirt and gravel roads follows the numerous spring-fed creeks in the Bears Paws. These roads are rife with streamside vegetation and quiet surprises, well worth the nagging doubts about route-finding that may accompany you.

4 Bears Paw

Highway 240 crosses the Milk River near Chinook and cuts south through wheatfields. Oil pumps seem an anomaly in this pastoral setting, yet there they are—like large sluggish insects bobbing their heads up and down, up and down, slurping the resinous goo stockpiled underground. Plowed furrows aim directly toward each pump, then circle around and angle back to continue the original line. From the air they must look like bull's-eyes scattered across the fields.

The rich natural resources beneath the soil reveal the frenetic geologic past of this stolid landscape. Sandstone and shale deposits slid around atop volcanic ash that had weathered into bentonite. The impermeable shale on top trapped vast reservoirs of natural gas and oil beneath it. This particular entrapment is called the Bowes Field. It has a total of 57 oil wells and 38 gas wells, though not all are producing.

Bentonite is commonly called "gumbo," and motorists who encounter the substance after a rainstorm can easily imagine massive blocks of land sliding around on it as blithely as their one-ton pickups do.

Sixteen miles south of Chinook, a state park commemorates the last battle between Chief Joseph's Nez Perce and the United States military. When I visited in June, the grass was so severely burned that the stubby root clumps disintegrated underfoot with a pathetic, scratching sound. Charred, skeletal trees backdropped the markers memorializing that doomed Indian encampment. The wind found nothing to rustle and sway in its passage.

It seemed somehow fitting that a prairie fire had so completely consumed the Chief Joseph Bears Paw Battlefield State Park. This was where the last of a noble tribe were consumed by misguided political policies; where the good-faith surrender of a besieged people was betrayed.

I walked through the park, then stood in reflective solitude. Prairie dogs played tag, oblivious to my solemnity. Two motorcyclists with blaring radios jerked me back to the present. My annoyance turned to amusement when I saw the riders—two paunchy, gray-haired fellows. They turned off their Harleys and I moseyed over for a chat.

One had just retired, after 41 years with the railroad. He'd been to the East Coast for a visit, and said he had to come back and get out on the plains again. "Yup," he stated. "There's nothin' like sitting right here looking out at nothing. The trees were pretty for a while, but I couldn't stand it back there. Everywhere you go, there's forty thousand people waiting to run over you."

Highway 240 is paved as far as Cleveland. The entrance to the Cleveland Bar is shaded by a tangle of hops vines. Inside, the bartender was a one-man show for the assembled imbibers: two irrigators; a couple from North Dakota who professed having absolutely no idea how they ended up on this road; a pair of locals; and later, the two motorcyclists. Soft drinks, beers, coffee, or whiskeys softened our dry throats. Stories and laughter kept us there, entertained and grateful for a respite from the glare and heat outside.

Cleveland sits on the eastern edge of the Bears Paws. Bearpaws. Bear's Paw. Bear Paw. Bearpaw. Bears Paws. No one seems to agree on the "correct" name, nor even from what exact vantage point it looked like some massive paw of *Ursus* spread out on the prairie.

Geologists agree, however, that about 50 million years ago this isolated range was lifted from beneath, pushed up out of the surrounding plains until it finally erupted. Much of the dark volcanic rock jutting like steep spines out of the grassy hillsides is known as shonkinite. Shonkinite probably oozed from about 200 miles below the earth's surface and is found few places in the world outside of central Montana.

A network of dirt and gravel roads follows the numerous spring-fed creeks in the Bears Paws. These roads are rife with streamside vegetation and quiet surprises, well worth the nagging doubts about route-finding that may accompany you. Ducks paddle in the puddled potholes; truly picturesque farms and ranches really do dot the countryside; incredible cloud formations spiral up, caught in the updrafts created by a surprised wind accustomed to whipping straight across the prairie.

Painted Lady butterflies sip nectar from roadside wildflowers; mom, dad, the kids, and the dogs urge their cows along the road from one pasture to another; cross-country runners train on the hilly roads through the Rocky Boy's Reservation. Beaver Creek Park provides a lovely oasis from the arid prairie.

Past residents' deep attachment to their history in these hills is evident. Black steel rods frame an outline of a tiny church keeping watch over a small cemetery at the top of Hungry Hollow Road. A barely noticeable cement marker on Clear Creek Road notes the location of the vanished Bear Paw post office and store. Historic markers sketch the history of an abandoned homestead.

Stop a lot. Smell the moisture, which is rare along the Hi-Line. Watch for marmots and deer and hawks. Listen to the birds and crickets. Feast your eyes on the soft greenery of this oasis.

Few of the roads in the Bears Paws are marked—have a full tank of gas, good local maps, and a compass. And make certain your vehicle is reliable, to avoid our situation:

Four P.M.: Hungry Hollow Road in the Bears Paw Mountains. Hot summer day. We have a major vehicle breakdown. The last ranch was about two miles back, so we decide to walk forward in hopes that a nearer place might lie in that direction.

Five P.M.: Still walking. We were wrong. There is obviously no hurry, so we lie down beside a stream and watch the funnels and drifts of cirrus clouds throw shadows on squat piles of cumulus clouds. Twin funnels twine around each other, and sprout into triplets. Mares' tails reach over the horizon. It's a show I'd pay admission to see.

Five-thirty P.M.: A rancher picks us up and takes us farther down the road to his grandparents' place. There I telephone for help, and we are treated to conversation, cool drinks

and leftover anniversary cake. Four-hundred-seventy-five friends came here a few days ago to help Bill and Una Young celebrate fifty years of marriage. The revelers consumed an entire barbecued cow and a roast pig, as well as untold gallons of potato salad and other fixin's. I am glad they left a few pieces of cake for us. The Youngs are wonderfully hospitable to us, their unbidden guests.

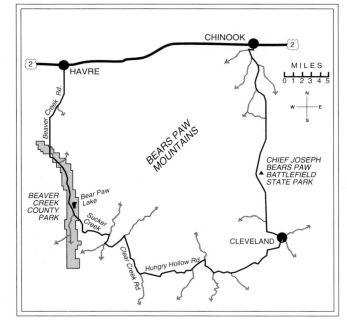

Six-thirty P.M.: A Montana highway patrolman stops by and we ride together to the vehicle. He radios the towing company, to find they have gone up the wrong drainage. He gives clear, precise directions.

Seven-thirty P.M.: Still no tow truck. We're only forty-some miles from town. The patrolman radios the truck crew again. They have once again taken a wrong road, and are about fifty miles away now. Fifty dirt-road miles. We dig into the cooler for snacks, and swap stories with the patrolman. He covers an area encompassing 500 square miles, but the highways tonight are quiet and we're glad he's around.

Nine-thirty P.M.: We don sweaters and long pants—the breeze is cool. Once again the patrolman radios for the truck crew's whereabouts. Once again, he learns they are still driving. This time, it seems, towards us.

Ten-thirty P.M.: I perk up at the hoot of an owl, follow the sound down the road in the darkness, listen, and wonder who it calls. Montana's owls range from the pygmy owl, which would fit on the palm of your hand, to great gray owls with wingspans of five feet. Who is this one calling quietly in the darkness? Perhaps its hoot is the owl equivalent of a song to celebrate the night.

Headlights shimmer on the road. It turns out to be the

The American and Canadian border guards in Hands Across the Border, *by Montana sculptor Lyndon Pomeroy, symbolize the friendship between the two countries. The Havre park is the scene of ceremonies, and always a focal point during Festival Days, which are held in late September.*

rancher who picked us up, on his way home from grandma's. We chat, laugh a bit, then he's on his way.

Eleven P.M.: The stars are brilliant. One more set of headlights bobs into sight, this time with yellow warning lamps across the top of the cab. We're almost too tired to rejoice.

One A.M.: The patrolman drops us at a motel in Havre. Blessed sleep.

Havre is the seat of government for Hill County. It's a commercial center for area agriculture, and home to Northern Montana College. "Haverites" flock to Fresno Reservoir for summer water sports and winter ice skating and fishing. The community's location can be a mixed blessing to residents: the Milk River contributes innumerable mosquitoes to summer barbecues, but the eternal Hi-Line wind keeps the bulk of those buzzing blood-suckers at bay.

Residents seem proud of the region's varied history. They speak enthusiastically of the Wahkpa Chu'an buffalo jump site, of Fort Assinniboine, of honyockers and cowboys.

Grit, Guts and Gusto: A History of Hill County, a publication of the Hill County Bicentennial Commission, has some very entertaining reading. Havre, originally called Bull Hook Bottoms after a nearby creek, has a true Wild West past full of outlaws, bootlegging, and tall stories. Early settlers had to protect their claims quickly with a fence, and wire was often in short supply. One tale in the book relates, "There was a long fence belonging to a big cattle company—fair game in any case—and I decided to 'borrow' the top wire from a stretch of this. I was working along, quietly, up a hill. I'd pull out the staples for two or three posts, roll the wire to that point, then go staple-pulling again. Presently I began to notice, once in a while, a tug on the wire I was working on. I couldn't understand it, so I crawled up to the top of the hill and looked over. What I saw plumb amazed me. Coming up the opposite slope of the hill, swiping the same wire I was working on, was the —— preacher of the town of ——."

WAYNE SCHERR

BEVERLY R. MAGLEY

Above: *A painted lady butterfly sips the nectar of wild hesperus blossoms.*
Left: *Chief Joseph Bears Paw Battlefield.*

Another story in the book tells of a June 1906 storm in which four-inch hailstones killed stock as winds demolished windows, lifted automobiles and their passengers, and un-roofed buildings.

For a more recent perspective of Havre, I contacted life-long resident Rob Kiesling. Walking up his driveway, I saw where a yellow-bellied sapsucker had made a perfect ring of holes in the Austrian pine. A stump of petrified redwood from the Bearspaws sat among the planters surrounding the door-way. A flicker was working on the house siding, tap-tap-tapping a lively percussive rhythm outside the kitchen windows.

Rob and Helen Kiesling sat with me at their kitchen table, sipping coffee while I prompted Rob's encyclopedic recall of information about the Havre area. He spoke of the drouth and Depression in 1932, when the grasshoppers migrated through. "I remember looking at them in the sky," he reminisced. "Their wings glittered in the sun. The wind was coming from the north, and they created their own dust cloud that covered town as they flew over."

In the 1990s drouth is again a critical factor, and Havre is facing major changes in its economy. With a double whammy of drouth and the railroad transferring 190 jobs elsewhere, it's a community in transition. But the Kieslings believe that adversity builds character. "Those that stay are strong survivors, and we celebrate it," said Helen. "Havre has never had it easy."

The Kieslings know firsthand about adversity. They were engaged when Rob left for active duty in France during WWI. He returned home completely blind. Nevertheless, they married, had five children and moved to Billings to continue their educations. Helen attended her own classes and also accompanied Rob to his so she could take notes for him. She read his economics and philosophy textbooks aloud to him each night, and kept up with her own assignments for completing a master's degree in nursing. They finished school and jumped at the chance to move back to Havre, where Helen directed the nursing program at Northern Montana College for more than twenty years.

"When I first moved here, I thought I had come to the ends of the earth," Helen laughed. "No trees. No water. But I learned to love it. I'm so glad we live here and raised our family here. Now when we go across the Divide I can hardly wait to get back to the sunshine and big skies. We're here to stay."

5 Sweetgrass Hills

High-schoolers' penchants for writing their graduation years in a prominent place simply cannot be thwarted. While we're all accustomed to seeing the year outlined in white rocks on a hillside, or painted on the town water tower, Chester's seniors had to punt. No hill. No overpass. No-no to defacing the grain silos. So they spray-painted it neatly on the highway and, I assume, graduated quite proudly in the appointed year.

A crew of fifteen people were cleaning the Methodist parsonage in Chester, to prepare for the new pastor. I picked my way past buckets, drapes, and ladders to find Darlene and Arlo Skari, who farm north of town.

The Skaris are members of the Sweetgrass Hills Protective Association, a group of ranchers, Native Americans, and local citizens fighting to protect the pure water and traditional sacred lands from the threat of heap-leach gold mining. The Bureau of Land Management has designated the hills an Area of Critical Environmental Concern—nevertheless they are vulnerable to potential road-building and exploratory drilling that could permanently disrupt the aquifers.

"These are the only hills in the entire county. Their springs feed three major water systems for us," Arlo said. "We can't survive here without our source of clean water."

Arlo is a certified pharmacist, Darlene a teacher. Neither would leave farming. "There's an advantage to farming you can't find in other jobs," Arlo stated. "When it's time to work, you just throw away the clocks and calendar and give it your full effort. But when the work is done, you have blocks of time to do whatever you want."

"I like the distances and the bigness of the plains," Darlene said. "The wind drives me crazy but it also brings the most beautiful cloud formations."

The Skaris went to the University of Montana last winter quarter to challenge themselves with philosophy, psychology, and religion courses. They also like to hike in Glacier National Park, and that presents a different sort of a challenge to Arlo.

"I have no trouble climbing a silo," he laughed. "But I'm really a flatlander at heart. I just freeze on those mountain faces."

Chester is a county seat in the core of Montana's fertile, productive region called The Golden Triangle—stellar dryland grain-growing country. The community (population 942) has several distinctions for a small Montana town. For one, there are more churches than bars. For another, the town has an arts council and a public art center with changing displays. Residents sponsor dinner theater with the Vigilante Players, Shakespeare in the Parks, and performances in other arts. Philip Aaberg, nationally renowned pianist/composer, grew up in Chester.

The list goes on. Volunteers staff a museum. Chester boys and girls have won their share of basketball and volleyball championships. There are clubs to keep busy with every night of the week—Rotary, Photography, Garden, Lions, Jaycees, Genealogy, Great Books, and more. The Hi-Line Chuckwagon Band performs oldies on home-made instruments, accompanied by stories and old-time humor. Nearly all members of the band are in their 70s or 80s, which accounts for some of the funniest instruments, like the "pan-jo," made from a bedpan.

This level of community activity and involvement continues a long tradition in Chester. In 1913 the community had 200 fewer residents, but nevertheless boasted an opera house and two weekly newspapers. The homesteading and ranching history of this region is now displayed in the Liberty County Museum, and written about at length in *Our Heritage*, a 500-page compilation of Liberty County anecdotes and remembrances published for the 1976 Bicentennial celebration.

Our Heritage discloses a mosaic of hopes, hardships, and humor. Helen Albright of Chester tells of pushing a baby in a buggy five miles across the bumpy prairie. Eva Strode Melvin reminisces about dances in Whitlash where there were ten boys to every girl; about her father giving a young troublemaker "a whole wood shed full of psychiatry on the seat of learning"; of their clothes-eating goat who butted everyone until "it was worth your life to bend over."

The backroads route circles the Sweetgrass Hills north of Chester. Don't drive this route when it's wet. In fact, don't go if it's even damp, because the dirt roads here develop their own topography in response to moisture. Miniature canyons, waterways, cliffs, and mountains impede the vehicle, complete with impromptu water reservoirs, and mudslides that cascade down the ruts. It would be entertaining for a geology class to walk here and study erosion and mountain building, but driving it wet is less than fun.

Do drive this route on a dry day, however, because it is a wonderful journey encircling a unique spot in Montana. The Sweetgrass Hills claim center stage, outshining the tiny community of Whitlash, the Sage Creek Hutterite Colony, and the old homesteader shacks flanked by innumerable acres of wheat and pasture.

The Sweetgrass Hills aren't hills at all. Nor are they even a related grouping. Each of the three main buttes is actually a small mountain range of sedimentary rocks wrapped around an igneous core. Today, they thrust up out of a sea of wheat; 70,000 to 130,000 years ago they jutted up through a sea of glacial ice.

Dwarfed by the immensity of the surrounding plains, the buttes appear deceptively small. However, they host freshwater springs, forest, grasslands, wildflowers, elk, and deer. East Butte rises to nearly 7,000 feet and covers thirty square miles. Middle, or Gold Butte, was the site of a brief frenzy of gold mining in the 1880s. West Butte is an isolated, rounded knob with forested slopes. Smaller, eye-catching Haystack Butte sits a bit south of the larger buttes, its near-perfect conical shape like a blip on a cardiogram.

Little, if any, sweet grass grows in these hills. The nomenclature derives either from an inaccurate translation of the Indian name for the hills, "sweet pine," or from an early settler's description of abundant "sweet" grazing in the region.

The wheatfields are plowed and planted to within an inch of the roads. Creative plowing is evidenced by the swirls and twirls of furrows in the puckered foothills on the north slopes of the hills. I would like to see those farmers make their tractors pirouette—they must laugh while successfully navigating the steeper dips and rises.

This is a land of patterns, the sky a burst of free-form creativity above the striking geometric angles on the land. Dappled sunlight plays with the colors of fallow fields and ripening wheat. An immense, shallow cloud bank comes in low from the north to neatly cut off the tops of each butte, while a lukewarm blue sky hesitates above. Pronghorn antelope pose, silhouettes against the sky, framed by the Sweetgrass Hills. Pale gold wheat is luminous beneath roiling deep gray clouds.

The sky. It rivets your attention, adding brilliant hues of orange, red, gold, and crimson to the horizon at daybreak, and again at dusk. The sky here is magnificent—expanding life's possibilities.

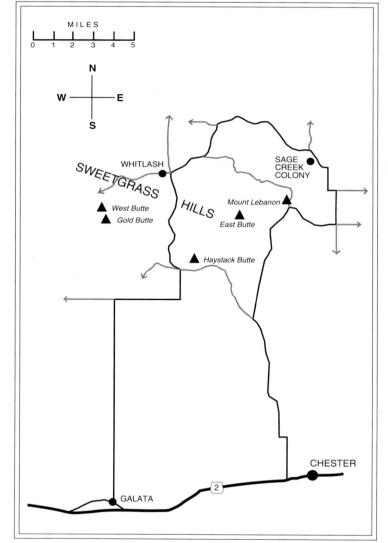

Above: *The church in Whitlash.*
Right: *Even the cattle guards have a personal touch in the Sweetgrass Hills.*

Facing page: *Hi-Line sunset.*

6 Chalk Buttes– Medicine Rocks

Southeast Montana. Arid, seared grasses. Parched stream-beds and badlands. Shades of tan neutralizing the subtle contours of the land.

Dust swirled in through the car's air vents, settled on the dashboard, obscured the instrument panel, coated my sunglasses. Dust in my eyes, on my lap, up my nose.

It's hard to look out on the high plains and envision a vast marsh here 75 million years ago. Harder still to envision dinosaurs slogging through muck, drooling as they munched the sodden vegetation. One more stretch of the imagination is required to comprehend that the bones of those very dinosaurs were preserved in the dry sandstone and shale south of present-day Ekalaka. Perhaps the term "bone-dry" originated here, an arid area rich in well-preserved fossils.

Ekalaka is a traveler's respite after driving through those surrounding plains. Low hills support scrubby trees and provide some relief from the unrelenting browns. Strikingly white cliffs gird the pine-topped Chalk Buttes. Aspens shade campsites in Ekalaka Park. Springfed creeks trickle down slopes.

Ekalaka was named for the Oglala Sioux woman Ijkalaka ("Swift One"), niece of Sitting Bull and wife of the first permanent white settler, D.H. Russell. Ijkalaka's descendants still live in the area.

The town looks like many others. The two-block main street sports the only pavement. There are a few watering holes, a few cafes with the usual slate of fried everything, a few places to stay. A few public telephones testify to the fact that this is a county seat.

What's not usual about Ekalaka is its museum and the director. Carter County Museum and Marshall Lambert are nearly synonymous. Which is not to downplay the innumerable hours volunteered by county residents. Lambert has spearheaded the creation of one of the most remarkable small museums in our nation. After working in the spare corners of the high school basement, he now creates displays in a 6,000-square-foot museum building.

The museum is a converted garage, where Lambert and a friend built massive interior rock walls of petrified wood to separate the display areas. The petrified wood came from rangeland in this region. The color and texture variations make the walls intriguing.

An assortment of Indian artifacts and early settlers' paraphernalia adorns several display areas. The tower someday will hold an eternally swinging pendulum. Walk past these attractions to the back of the museum and be confronted by a broad assortment of dinosaur, marine, and mammal bones.

Lambert mounted a complete skeleton of an *Anatosaurus* (duck-billed dinosaur) that measures 16 feet tall and 35 feet long. "It was like assembling a three-dimensional jigsaw puzzle," Lambert said. "My predecessor collected the bones, and I put it together."

A gigantic *Triceratops* skull sits nearby. A notecard mentions that this several-ton beast had only a two-pound brain. A few calculations tell me that the *Triceratops* brain comprised about five one-thousandths of its mass. Human brains, by contrast, comprise about 2 percent of our mass. But don't feel smug yet: a spider monkey's brain is nearly five percent of its mass. On the you-are-as-smart-as-your-brain-is-large scale, that puts monkeys well above humans. After reading the morning news, many days I'm inclined to agree.

Various bones and fragments sit displayed on pieces of paper once intended to record baseball scores and pitching statistics. "This is a home-grown affair here," stated Lambert. "There are always exhibits to work on and projects to finish."

Lambert collected the first-ever skull of a new genus and species of dinosaur, the *Nanotyrannus* "bonehead" dinosaur. "We still don't know what its body may have looked like,"

Lambert commented. "No one has ever found a skull and skeleton together." A cast of the skull is displayed behind glass. Mastodon teeth lie next to a mammoth pelvis and a 10.5-foot-long tusk.

Lambert retired in 1975, after 34 years of full-time teaching. This "retirement" is a labor of love. I found him at the museum on his day off, writing an article about the need to standardize laws regarding fossil-collecting on federal lands. "[Fossils] are a nonreplaceable resource," he stated. "People are digging them up and selling them and we're losing opportunities to learn new things from them." Presently, Lambert is excavating another skeleton south of town. He has found most of the hind leg bones, as well as foot and toe bones. He's reasonably sure it's another *Hadrosaur* (duck-billed dinosaur family), but the excitement lies in wondering if it may be a new species. "I've identified some skeletal differences already," Lambert said. "You just never know until it's all uncovered."

Medicine Rocks State Park lies twelve miles north of Ekalaka. Once a holy place of Native Americans, it is now a place where visitors can drive between odd sandstone formations. Some rise to eighty feet—nearly all are severely pockmarked by the relentless wind. In time, the wind will erode the abundant human graffiti just as it is eroding the rocks themselves.

Look for the crossbedding in the rocks: those thin striations map the prehistoric winds that blew and shifted grain after grain of ancient sand dunes.

Most of the roads around and in Ekalaka have a dirt or gravel surface. A scenic loop through the Ekalaka Hills and around the Chalk Buttes is no exception. The eastern half of the loop provides pleasant scenes of hills, hay meadows, ranches, and pastures. It's particularly pretty with the bright greens or golds of spring or fall.

Stop at the Mill Iron Store to chat with Emmett and Jean Harmon. Chances are, several locals will also be enjoying their cheery company and coffee. Jean makes a great pot of soup, and every pie is baked from scratch. "The neighbors keep me supplied with rhubarb," Jean said. There's usually apple, pumpkin, or cherry pie, too. One loyal fan begs for chocolate pie, and she'll make that also, if he promises to come every day and have a piece until it's finished.

The Harmons are the kind of folks you just feel good about meeting. Emmett was a construction worker and the couple lived all over the country. Now they're staying put. "Mill Iron is the homiest place I've ever lived," Emmett said. "This is as pretty a piece of the state that there is."

The Harmons bought the Mill Iron Store in 1980 and ran it for ten years before deciding to really retire. They spent two years living near grandchildren in North Dakota, but missed Mill Iron so much they moved back and reopened in 1992.

"The people here are really exceptional," Jean said. "We love living here and enjoy having people come over, so we may as well keep the place open."

The decor is simple and straightforward. A curved counter and several round tables make for easy conversation. The Harmons' son made the large wooden cowboy sculptures that are in the dining area and on the boardwalk outside. You can sit at the counter and watch Emmett or Jean make your lunch in the kitchen.

Hunting season is their busiest. Jean cooks large, family-style meals. "You can't believe how much some of those people can eat!" she exclaimed.

Emmett converted two large trailers into sleeping rooms and added Western-style wooden false fronts to dress them up a bit. Hunters and travelers stay in those simple lodgings out back.

The Mill Iron Store. It's not actually a store—it's a cafe with comfortable conversation and a few odds and ends available for purchase.

The sun sank completely behind the horizon and lit the entire western sky in a surreal lemon-yellow. Rosy-pink beams launched straight overhead and faded into the remaining pale blue patch of sky. The profiles of the hills and buttes were softened, golden, luminous, while their blue-gray shadows stretched out a half mile and evaporated in the treeless expanses.

BEVERLY R. MAGLEY

The loop south of Ekalaka encircles the Chalk Buttes. Pershing Cutoff Road stays low, cutting across flat expanses of farmland. Views south extend incredible distances. To the north, trees sprout atop the Chalk Buttes like crewcuts.

Drive west on the Powderville Road for about three miles. The extensive view westward from the top of the rise shows numerous small buttes and badlands rising from the arid plains, the dinosaur country that Marshall Lambert is exploring.

I watched an unforgettable sunset from that spot on the Powderville Road. The sun sank completely behind the horizon and lit the entire western sky in a surreal lemon-yellow. Rosy-pink beams launched straight overhead and faded into the remaining pale blue patch of sky. The profiles of the hills and buttes were softened, golden, luminous, while their blue-gray shadows stretched out a half mile and evaporated in the treeless expanses.

JOHN REDDY

DAVID MUSSER

Above: *Chalk Buttes.*
Right: *Distinctive pockmarked rock formation at Medicine Rocks State Park.*

Facing page, left: *Spring Creek between Powderville and Ekalaka.*
Right: *Marshall Lambert and "friend" at the Carter County Museum.*

7 Tongue River–Northern Cheyenne Reservation

The Northern Cheyenne are surrounded, and they are fighting for their lives. Strip mines, coal-fired generating plants, railroads, and transmission lines press from every side. Coal companies come courting the poverty-stricken tribe with promises of millions of dollars. But the Cheyennes have resisted, and fight for clean air and clean water. They fight to preserve the cultural fabric of their lives.

"You grow up with the struggles," acknowledged Gail Small. "If we lose a bout, the kids will take it on. We'll continue to fight for the survival of our culture and our homeland. Our people walked here from Oklahoma with no shoes. They knew they needed this land. History gives us the strength to make good decisions for future generations."

Small is a lawyer and the director of Native Action, a nonprofit organization in Lame Deer that works for social, environmental, and economic justice for Native Americans. The organization identifies and works on critical issues facing the tribe. The challenges in 1992 were getting banks to provide credit, defending the integrity of the homeland against environmental degradation, and fighting for a high school in Lame Deer.

One by one, the Northern Cheyennes are winning their battles, setting national precedents for using legal means to obtain equality and fairness. Small and her husband Joe Rodriguez, also a lawyer, speak around the nation about the issues and battles.

"Our tie to the land goes back to ancient times," Small said. "The circle of life continues here through the Creator and our lives. We won't give that away."

West of Lame Deer, a monument above the Busby trading post commemorates Two Moons, who led the Cheyennes against Custer. Below, a concrete tipi next to the highway is disintegrating, lending a bleak aspect to the area. The post does a steady business in pop, chips, burgers, and other odds and ends. It is a dismal-looking place, but the white proprietor seemed oblivious to his surroundings as he hummed Native American songs, greeted the children fondly, flipped burgers, and chatted cheerily with the customers.

The backroads route on Highway 314 goes nearly to Wyoming. Willows and cottonwoods are thick along Rosebud Creek; coulees cut deep swathes into the low red and tan hills; cattle graze in the pastures.

Yet another of Montana's backroads surprises not marked on the map is Rosebud State Monument. The Battle of the Rosebud was one of the largest Indian battles in United States history, with nearly 3,000 fighters. Chief Spotted Wolf led Sioux and Cheyenne warriors against General Crook's troops and Crow and Shoshoni warriors.

The magnitude of this battle has been eclipsed by the Battle of the Little Bighorn, fought eight days later on the other side of the Rosebud Mountains. The Sioux and Cheyennes honed their fighting skills here before going on to defeat Custer.

Meadowlarks sang and the breeze rustled the grass at the battlefield. Walk a mile or so up the primitive road. You'll find an extensive view of the surrounding area, and solitude for contemplating the bloody history enacted here.

This is coal country. Three huge seams of valuable bituminous coal covering hundreds of square miles lie beneath the surface. Experts estimate that there are more than two billion tons of coal yet to be mined. And the big mining companies are working hard to get as much as possible out right now.

Huge slag piles outline the strip mines around Decker. Drag lines, the lines of railroad tracks, and powerlines march off in various directions. Spring Creek Coal company announces its mining location with a freshly painted sign on a shovel twelve people could stand in. The Decker Coal Company logo shows two flying—or fleeing?—Canada geese.

Decker has a post office/store, and a grammar school. And the mines. No homes, no businesses, no civic pride. But it is no future ghost town, unlike Montana's earlier mining boom locations. Miners generally live 25 miles south in Sheridan, Wyoming, and commute to work. For visitors, it's worth driving to the little Decker school, which overlooks an immense expanse of landscape and provides some perspective on the magnitude of the mines.

The county road leading northeast out of Decker climbs atop the hills and provides vistas over the desertscape of southeast Montana. It looks so similar to the high plains desert of Utah and Arizona that I wondered what extraordinary slickrock canyons were lying hidden beneath the surface, awaiting exposure and exploration some millennium in the future.

The road winds along the tops of the hills in this land of browns, beiges, tans, and muted sage-greens, then drops down to the Tongue River. Pronghorn antelope were abundant; a Wall Drug sign hung on a post; the heat shimmered in waves; deer grazed with Black Angus bulls; the local road crew had piled rock slabs into the biggest cairn I've ever seen.

The sun glittered through the reddish dust trailing my vehicle. There could be no sneaking around here—the dust hung in the air for miles behind, accurately marking the route.

Mark Nance ranches along the Tongue River. He started coming here as a child, when his mother pinned express tags to his shirt so train conductors could help him make connections between his home in Mississippi and his relatives here in Montana.

Nance finds the ranching community around here to be in a state of real flux. "There are those adamantly for selling the land and letting them mine the coal, and there are those adamantly against it," he said. "And there aren't many in between. It seems that the older ones are for, and the younger against. Maybe that's because the older ranchers have been broke once or twice, and the younger ones haven't felt that yet."

We sat on the airy screened-in porch of Nance's log home, and he told stories, one about coming home a day in 1951 and announcing to his wife that he had bought a house. The only catch was, it was about 15 miles away. They cut it into three pieces, hauled it to their property and put it back together. Then Nance bought a little sawmill and built a second story on their house.

It's a homey, attractive place, and you'd never know it was once cut into pieces. The master bedroom is furnished with Buffalo Bill's guestroom set; hand-made chairs surround the long dining-room table; the ranch-style furnishings are comfortable.

Nance likes the freedom of ranching more than any other aspect. "It's no eight-to-five job," he stated. "It can be very long hours, or good blocks of time off. It's a challenge to make money in the cattle business. But as long as you get a decent income and have this freedom, I don't know of anything to compare with it."

St. Labre (lah-BRAY) Indian School in Ashland has operated continuously since 1884, and continues to educate the Native American population. The visitor center has a small gallery and an excellent museum display of Plains Indians' tools and clothing. The beadwork and handiwork on the items is fantastic.

I half-watched the short video presentation explaining the history of this Jesuit mission. The other half of my attention was focused unabashedly on the phone conversation of a staffperson who blended English and Pueblo words into fascinating rhythms and singsong cadences.

St. Labre clearly tries to honor both its Catholic roots and its Native American culture. The church has a Christian cross merged into the top of a tipi-shaped steeple. The school building under construction incorporates native geometric designs into the brickwork. Teachers and students crossed the grassy campus; visitors strolled around the grounds; the Tongue River flowed silently nearby. Here is a place that demonstrates hope and commitment to the future of the Northern Cheyennes.

Coal companies come courting the poverty-stricken tribe with promises of millions of dollars. But the Cheyennes have resisted, and fight for clean air and clean water. They fight to preserve the cultural fabric of their lives.

Left: *The church at St. Labre Indian School shows the blend of cultures.* BEVERLY R. MAGLEY

Below: *Room with view, Tongue River Valley.*
TIMOTHY EAGAN

Facing page: *Tongue River.* TIMOTHY EAGAN
Inset: *Red shale found around Ashland.* JOHN REDDY

The other half of my attention was focused unabashedly on the phone conversation of a staffperson who blended English and Pueblo words into fascinating rhythms and singsong cadences.

Beartooths–
8 Crow Reservation

Hardin retains strong connections to Native American traditions and the Old West. The Rendezvous Musical Variety Show runs nightly throughout the summer and features music and dance acts from Northern Plains tribes, as well as from the Navaho, Zuni, Pueblo, Creek, and Mohawk nations. Once a year, Little Big Horn Days features a reenactment of Custer's Last Stand, with Native American and white actors portraying historic events at nearby Little Bighorn Battlefield.

Walt Secrest of Hardin epitomizes the local interest in cowboying and white settlement of the West. He spent over 40 years working as a rodeo pickup man—the one who helps the competitive rider dismount—all over the West. That stopped after his neck broke when his horse fell on him during a cattle roundup.

He retained his connection to Western history, however, and now writes cowboy poetry and keeps Old West outfits—not the kind of outfits you wear—the kind movie producers need: eight-horse hitches, longhorn cattle, covered wagons, matched teams of horses, and bullwhips. Secrest furnishes outfits for wagon trains, parades, movies, and various celebrations. When you see a matched pair of red or blue roans pulling a wagon across the silver screen, or down Main Street, Montana, chances are good that they're Secrest's stock.

Hardin's Bighorn County Historical Museum exhibits are carefully researched and well-displayed, and volunteers have restored numerous buildings from the turn of the century. You can walk through the old Corinth Store and Post Office, remember getting full-service gas at an old filling station, see the blacksmith tools in the barn, and imagine cooking on the wood stove in the farmhouse. The museum sponsors an annual Country Fun Weekend.

Hardin exhibited the lack of trendiness and community involvement of rural Montana life. A poster for Crisis Hot Line help was next to a placard advertising the Undercover Gals' Quilt Show. Locals of every description met at Dandy Tom's for excellent lunch and ice cream. According to an ad, the

sheep show dance proceeds were earmarked for local disaster relief. The local aerobics and workout studio disguised itself as The Dance Ranch, and exhibited saddles and tack instead of neon Lycra outfits in its display window.

Crow Fair and Powwow in Crow Agency is the largest Native American fair in Montana. Tipis encircle the main dance arena the third weekend of August every year. Participants and revelers share in parades, giveaways, rodeoing, feasts, competitive dancing, and general celebrating.

Yellowtail Dam impounds the Bighorn River, generating electricity and providing a constant source of water to downstream irrigators. Abundant water for irrigating has turned the flat, arid lowlands along the Bighorn River into fertile fields for growing sugar beets, alfalfa, grains, and livestock. It looked to be a quiet, rural existence. Tractors moved slowly across fields; a dog and horse trotted companionably down the middle of the street in Saint Xavier; pickup trucks were pulled over beside good fishing holes.

The big, gaily-painted boxes in the fields harbor leafcutter bees, important and effective pollinators of alfalfa. The bees are attracted to certain colors and patterns—hence the bold geometric designs on the boxes. Leafcutter bees are about one fourth the size of honeybees. They snip a dozen or more little circles from leaves, then shape the leaf pieces into a tiny thimble-shaped receptacle cell. The females stock each cell with pollen, nectar, and an egg, then seal the cell with more leaves. The larvae winter inside the cells and emerge in early June to pollinate the next crop of alfalfa.

Sugar beet harvest begins at the end of September. Growers along the Bighorn River haul their sweet crop to one of three stations. Each truck from Western Sugar then picks up over 62,000 pounds of beets to haul to the Billings sugar factory, in what looks like an unending procession.

I stopped at the Saint Xavier station. A constant stream of

Few fences and even fewer trees block the scene, presenting a satisfying vision of what this land must have looked like hundreds of years ago. Cutbanks show the meanders of occasional streams; intermittent gray and painted badlands claim your attention; you need only glance upward to see what the weather will be for the next few hours.

farm trucks delivered the sugary tubers. Shaking conveyer belts jiggled much of the dirt off, and each beet ended up atop an absolute mountain of other beets. Growers take their dirt back to their own fields, a guard against possible spread of soil diseases. The workers laughed when I exclaimed at the size of the pile, and told me that by the end of October the twenty-foot-high pile would completely cover several acres.

Sugar beets wouldn't win any beauty contests. But sure enough, if you break one in half there is very sweet juice inside. Not quite as sweet as raw sugar cane, but quite passably sweet. The bag of Western Sugar in my cupboard attests to its agreeable uses after processing.

Glorious. Splendid. Magnificent. These words touch on the beauty of Bighorn Canyon. A raptor has the best viewpoint, soaring at will between the steep canyon walls, or riding a thermal current to great heights to claim the big picture. The jagged cuts of the deep canyon envelope turquoise-blue waters, enclosing the river within the mountainous terrain before it is spilled out onto the prairie.

Those of us bound to the earth can still gain a sense of the scope and splendor of the region. The paved road to Ok-A-Beh near the dam, and the unimproved Forest Service road through the Pryor Mountains to Barry's Landing on the west side, provide panoramic views of the canyon, and beyond to the surrounding Pryor and Bighorn Mountains.

The Bighorn River originates as the Wind River in Wyoming, flows north and changes names, and eventually empties into the Yellowstone. It carved this canyon through the mountain layers of limestone and dolomite. Limestone, which is composed of calcium carbonate, was once the coral reefs and marine shells in a gigantic inland sea. These immense layers of material were eventually compressed into rock and pushed up to form the mountains.

Ten thousand years ago, prehistoric peoples inhabited this region. More recently, the Crow tribe lived and hunted

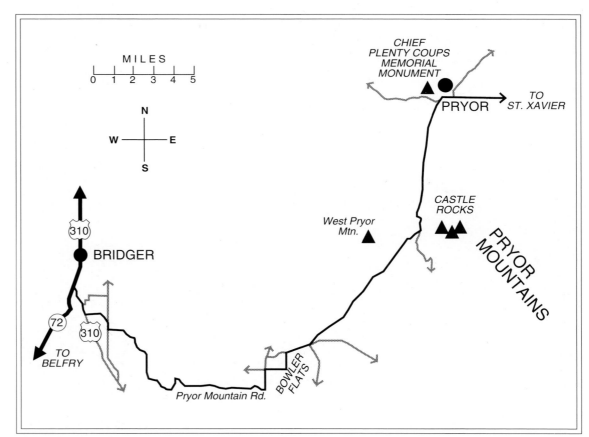

here. Ancient and contemporary sacred and ceremonial sites exist throughout the mountains and canyon.

Theo Hugs is the Indian Liaison Officer for Bighorn Canyon National Recreation Area. She acts as a bridge between the white world of the park and the Crow world. The two are sometimes worlds apart. In 1992, the hottest issue was a proposed trans-park road connecting Barry's Landing to Fort Smith. Crow

traditionalists opposed the road, wanting to protect the abundant cultural resources along the route; whites wanted the road for quicker access to recreation opportunities on the lake. Hugs' job was to let each side know the other's perspective.

"It's not an easy responsibility sometimes," she admitted. "The worlds are really different."

Hugs is a full-time park ranger, but after hours and on weekends she helps her husband on their ranch. They raise cattle, wheat, and hay. She also beads Crow designs from the mid-1800s into collars and forehead ornaments for horses, and makes beaded clothing for special occasions.

"It's our custom to exchange wedding outfits. The bride's family gives the groom his complete outfit, and the groom's family gives the bride hers. It's a big job, but lots of relatives help out, too."

Hugs said lots of people also help each other out at branding time. Typically, her family gets up at 4:30 A.M. to round up cattle and drive them to the branding corral before the day gets hot. Up to 75 neighbors and friends pull in about 8 A.M., and the work is finished by about 1 P.M. Generally, the men dehorn and castrate the calves, and women vaccinate and handle the branding iron. But some of the women enjoy roping and "wrassling" too.

When the work's all done, the ranch family supplies the meat for a big barbecue and everyone contributes to a potluck feast. Then it's time for volleyball, games, and visiting into the night. The next weekend it happens all over again, at the neighbor's ranch, and again the following weekend, and again, until everyone's calves are done.

"I like this area," Hugs stated. "I went away to college, but never really considered not returning. It's the people here—everyone helps each other. It's a good way to live."

The drive between Saint Xavier and Pryor is a delight. Immense tableaus of prairie and mountains are spread out for viewing as you top each rise. Few fences and even fewer trees

block the scene, presenting a satisfying vision of what this land must have looked like hundreds of years ago. Cutbanks show the meanders of occasional streams; intermittent gray and painted badlands claim your attention; you need only glance upward to see what the weather will be for the next few hours. I could drive this road every day and never tire of it.

Chief Plenty Coups State Monument near Pryor preserves Plenty Coups' log home and store, and the museum features Crow culture and history. The unimproved road south leads past burned-out houses and abandoned car carcasses, climbs under the beautiful Castle Rocks through Pryor Gap, and twists across the big fields on Bowler Flats. The descent down Pryor Mountain Road was lovely, past red buttes and green fields backdropped by the spectacular Beartooth Mountains on the western horizon.

Mounted fish, deer heads, and antelope heads kept watch over the canned goods at the Belfry store. The owner chatted about the quiet life here, and hand-stitched more squares for her Cathedral Window quilt. She grinned and said Belfry counted the cats and dogs to come up with a population of 250.

Growers here produce mainly sugar beets, corn, pinto beans, and, of course, cattle. You'll see a lot of cowboy hats silhouetted in the windows of passing pickups.

The sagebrush hill east of Bearcreek holds the local cemetery and a monument commemorating the men who died in Montana's worst coal mine disaster. An underground explosion in 1943 at the Smith Mine killed 74 miners and abruptly ended coal-mining in the area. The mine went from producing 500 tons of coal a day to being completely abandoned after the catastrophe. The deserted mine buildings alongside the highway are mute reminders of the tragedy.

The Bearcreek Saloon lures customers with gimmicks and fun. Patrons are loyal and entertained, whether racing pigs and iguanas, eating a celebration feed of buffalo roast and beef lips, or dancing to live music. It's a good bar, just plain fun.

The road climbs west towards Red Lodge. From the top of the hill, you can see hundreds of square miles of the desert-like landscape around the Pryor Mountains. It's a palette of subtle hues under the blue of the sky. The colors are

Above: Crow girl on horseback at Crow Fair parade.
Left: Crow dancers on float truck, Crow Agency.

Facing page: Bighorn River and the Bighorn Canyon National Recreation Area.

every shade of brown—chestnut, dun, ginger, mahogany, gold, tan, sienna, and bronze, the colors of a Russell Chatham painting.

Red Lodge was originally a camping place for Crow Indians. Large coal deposits brought immigrants to work the mines, and today the annual Festival of Nations celebrates the diverse ethnic heritage of the community.

Red Lodge is a year-round tourist town. Summer recreationists just off the famous Beartooth Highway are replaced by autumn hunters and hikers. Winter skiers give way to spring bicyclists and whitewater enthusiasts. A plethora of lodging opportunities supplements Main Street shops, galleries, restaurants, and antique stores serving the lucrative tourist trade. The dominant look is outdoorsy.

JK's store is stuffed with beads and trinkets, yarn, school notebooks, jewelry, and knickknacks. Photos of JK's family are thumbtacked to the walls. When he's not taking a long coffee break down at the Red Lodge Cafe, you can hang around his store and converse a while with this garrulous proprietor. With a little prodding, he'll pull out his accordion and serenade you with an old-time tune. It's a treat.

Kevin Red Star's eye-catching paintings are shown exclusively at Merida Gallery in Red Lodge. He had two pieces on tour in Europe in a show called The Cutting Edge of Creativity, and collectors all over the world display his artwork on their walls.

Red Star was born and raised in Lodge Grass. At age 16, he left to study art in Santa Fe, San Francisco, and New York City, but returned to live just north of Red Lodge, near his homeland.

"The essence of being a fine painter is drawing," Red Star stated. "First you have to learn to draw accurately. Then you can tear it apart, and know exactly what you're dissembling.

"I paint from what I know, what I grew up with. Summer encampments, weekend rodeos, mini-powwows," he contin-

ued. "I started to stylize fifteen years ago, and my art is always changing. There are so many things I want to paint and create. I may have a similar image from ten years ago, but the difference is reflected in what I've learned since then."

Highway 78 leads northwest along the edge of the Beartooth Mountains. A ten-mile loop into Luther leads even closer to the mountains, through attractive open ranchland littered with new homes. The mountains appear almost black with conifers; in the foreground, stands of aspen and cottonwood rise above the grasslands on the rolling hills.

Some places just don't need to advertise their wares because word of mouth from friend to friend does it all. Such is the case with the Grizzly Bar and Restaurant in Roscoe. Locals all point to this restaurant as the best place to eat in this whole region. Many of the Grizzly Restaurant fans drive down from Billings just for dinner. Build up your appetite and prepare for a feast of their award-winning beef dishes.

The backroads route follows Route 420 west from Absarokee, crosses the Stillwater River, then meanders northwest. It's a beautiful drive that begins in wide open rangeland, then descends into riparian habitats with interesting rock conglomerates and steep cliffs.

Another in-the-middle-of-nowhere historic marker appears along the route to note that this is part of the Bozeman Trail. I'm always mystified by who takes it upon themselves to erect a stout stone edifice, announcing facts to no one in particular, in the middle of a field far from any semblance of human life. It's a curious and delightful puzzle to ponder during those long, dusty drives on Montana's backroads.

You'll descend from huge fields of golden grasses with sweeping vistas of buttes, plains, and coulees, into an intimate canyon thick with shrubs and berries and cottonwoods crowded on the banks of Bridger Creek, between steep rock walls. Autumn colors through here are gorgeous. The backroads route ends at Exit 384 on Interstate 90.

Patrons are loyal and entertained, whether racing pigs and iguanas, eating a celebration feed of buffalo roast and beef lips, or dancing to live music. It's a good bar, just plain fun.

9 Crazy Mountains Loop

Gasahol—I upped my octane. Up yours. No thanks Iraq—I use ethanol/Make ethanol, not war—bring home the boys.

The receptionist and these bumperstickers greet you at the office of AlcoTech in Ringling. The brainchild of brothers Gordon and Jay Doig, this plant manufactures ethanol—pure 200 proof grain alcohol—from locally-grown wheat and barley. When added to gasoline, ethanol boosts the octane, reduces carbon monoxide emissions from the gasoline, and burns with no harmful by-products.

"We're probably the best-located plant, in terms of supply and demand," Gordon Doig said. "The grains grown here are excellent. We sell all over the West—Missoula, Idaho, Salt Lake City, Denver, Canada. I could send my total production to each one of those places, but it's good to keep a varied market. Portland alone would consume what twenty of my plants could produce."

Doig grew up in this valley, an area memorialized by his relative, author Ivan Doig. After a stint in the service, Gordon wanted to return home, and saw the potential for ethanol.

"When we started the business in 1981 the country was in its biggest energy crisis," he said. "We weathered it when crude dropped from $45 to $7 a barrel. It was a rough go. Now the demand is growing again. In fact, there's more demand than we can meet."

Every day, three or four loads of grain come to the plant by semi. Workers grind the grain nearly to flour, mix it with water to form a slurry, add enzymes and yeast, and manipulate the temperatures to convert the starch into sugar. Ethanol is one by-product of the process. Another is a highly-concentrated, high-protein fibrous supplement for dairy cows. Doig is also working with universities to develop food-grade items for his high-protein fiber. Nothing is wasted, and no harmful by-products or emissions released.

The plant employs eleven people, and contracts exclusively with about ten truckers who haul the grain in and the products out. The plant runs 24 hours a day, 365 days a year. "You can't tell that yeast to wait a minute while we go sleep," Doig laughed.

The ethanol is denatured, which basically means poisoned so it's unfit for human consumption. Doig says they looked into marketing the pure grain alcohol to the beverage industry, but opted not to. "That load of denatured ethanol out there in the truck sells for about $14,000," he said. "There's a $22 a gallon tax on consumable alcohol, so that means the taxes alone on that truckload would be $242,000. No thanks."

Highway 294 begins just north of Ringling and heads east to Martinsdale. Clusters of lupine bloomed between big clumps of sagebrush in the fields. I got up on a hilltop and looked around. Wispy, ragged bits of clouds trailed below the mass of solid clouds to the east. To the north, a few small clouds were scattered across a blue, blue sky over the Castle Mountains. The western sky was a brilliant, flat grayish-white, above the Big Belt Mountains. Lightning flashed and the straight lines of a hard rain traced the distance between thunderheads and earth over the Crazies to the south. An impressive panorama.

Turn off in Lennup for a seven-mile side trip to the ghost town of Castle. Fifteen hundred mining claims were worked here between 1886 and 1890, and the town had two hotels, a photo gallery, nine stores, a bank, churches, a schoolhouse, fourteen saloons (of course), four newspapers, and even a resident brass band. Castle's burgeoning life came to an abrupt end during the silver panic of 1893. Today, cow pies and grasshoppers mark the former main street. Rock foundations outline original buildings, and thistles and fireweed grow through the empty window frames. Some homes were built to last, and remain standing today.

Lee Rostad ranches near Lennup, where the Bozeman Fork and Warm Springs Creek merge to become the South Fork of the Musselshell River. "There are no real estate offices

Ten mule-deer bucks, from young spikes to a couple of big six-points, grazed on one side of the road. A herd of eight does grazed on the other side of the road. A marsh hawk soared low to the ground, searching for rodents. Snow in the cirques and couloirs in the Crazies formed a dramatic backdrop to the rolling, jutting golden topography in the foreground.

Downtown Livingston, a great place to explore architecture and/or restaurants.

time at first. For instance, at a dance the men all sat on one side and the women on the other. Well, I was good and tired of talk about babies so I went and sat with the men to talk about cows and hay. The whole place went dead quiet until I went back to the other side."

Rostad seems to have found her place in Lennup's social order since those early days. She is well-versed in area history and state politics. She writes the Cattle Women's Column for the newspaper in White Sulphur Springs and is the author of several books. Her newest, *Fourteen Cents and Seven Green Apples*, traces the history of the nearby Charles M. Bair family ranch.

Rostad is also a potter. She turns out functional pottery pieces in her Chicken House Pottery studio. The old log henhouse was a delightful hodgepodge of plates, bowls, tureens, and baking dishes in various stages of construction.

Rostad took pottery classes at the Archie Bray Foundation in Helena. "I tried to take the boys to high school in White Sulphur, but we got snowed in for two months and had to stay at the motel and eat TV dinners. So we decided to move me and the boys to Helena for the school year. I taught social studies, they went to school, and I learned to throw pots. Phil kept the ranch going here."

Martinsdale lies at the end of the road along the South Fork of the Musselshell. A dog lay sleeping in the middle of the main street, in no danger of any traffic except kids zooming around on bicycles. Yet another of Montana's eternal Mint Bars was adorned with yet another dozen mounted heads of deer. But across the street, Martinsdale has something a little different from most small towns in Montana. Good food.

The Crazy Mountain Inn is open every day during hunting season—October and November—and Wednesdays through Sundays the rest of the year. *Esquire* wrote that the Inn served the "best chicken-fried steak with cream gravy in the world." I don't know about that, but I do know they serve

here," she said. "Residents are mostly all third and fourth generation ranchers. If somebody sells out, the neighbors buy it."

Rostad was born in Roundup and attended the University of Montana. She spent time studying in England on a Fulbright Scholarship, then married Phil Rostad, a Lennup man. They lived a year in Japan before he brought his bride home to the family ranch.

"There's a pecking order here, like in any community. We have our leaders and our followers," she said. "I had a terrible

Above left: *Lutheran Church at Melville, and the Crazy Mountains.*
Above: *Backroad after rainstorm.*

good Mexican food the first and third Thursdays of each month; that the carrot-pineapple cake is excellent; and that the proprietors, Cheryl and Peter Marchi, are very friendly.

Three of their five kids were doing homework at the counter when I stopped in for lunch. We cleared a spot for me, and I learned that the line-up of ammunition behind the counter, just under the row of beer bottles, was contributed by customers. Ammo ranged in size from a 50-millimeter machine-gun bullet down to .22 shot. The bottles were mostly a mish-mash of American beers. An Australian brought the Victoria Bitter bottle; a smokejumper contributed Kessler's Smokejumper Beer 1940-1990; and somebody brought in a few Big Drive of '89 Coca-Cola bottles to complete the collection. An aquarium

on the other end of the counter held tropical fish to entertain those who are indifferent to ammo and bottles.

The Marchis bought the Crazy Mountain Inn several years ago and are methodically repairing and renovating. Peter was outside painting the frame of a leaded glass picture win-dow; Cheryl was cooking, and supervising homework. Each room upstairs is simply furnished with an antique bed and dresser. At $20/night per single, and good food in the cafe downstairs, it's a deal.

"This is a great place to raise a family," Cheryl stated. "We really do this business as a family. The older girls help us wait tables and haul wood. Peter and I cook. And we're always here for the youngest ones."

Farther east along the Musselshell, the Twodot Bar advertises itself as "Easy to Find—Hard to Leave." Past Twodot, the road jogs west around Porcupine Butte. With a little imagination, you can make out the outline of a head, body, and dragging tail, all furred (or firred) with scraggly stands of conifer quills.

Ten mule-deer bucks, from young spikes to a couple of big six-points, grazed on one side of the road. A herd of eight does grazed on the other side of the road. A marsh hawk soared low to the ground, searching for rodents. Snow in the cirques and couloirs in the Crazies formed a dramatic backdrop to the rolling, jutting golden topography in the foreground. A distinctive woo-oo-oo call came from the rimrocks above Sweetgrass Creek. A rock dove?

At his ranch along Otter Creek, Tack Van Cleve got us both a cup of coffee and settled back in his leather chair to tell me stories of his family and the Melville country. He's proud of the community, and cited the strong moral standards and the work ethic prominent among residents of this prosperous ranching area.

"Practically every ranch around here is run by fourth-generation ranchers," he said. "The church here is the oldest Lutheran congregation in Montana, organized in 1885. Our school is the largest rural school in the county. We called it the Settlement School when I went.

"I had the same teacher as my dad. We called her Aunt Signe, not Mrs. Anderson. Somebody figured out that ninety percent of Aunt Signe's students went on to graduate from college on the east or west coasts."

Van Cleve has a master's degree in guidance and education, and worked twelve years for Indian Affairs in Montana and Canada. "I loved teaching the Cheyennes in particular," he said. "Their way of thinking is very forthright. They have a real genuine quality about them."

He returned to run the ranch when his father, Spike, wanted to stop ranching and devote full time to writing books. "We're all raised that the ranch comes first," he stated. "It's traditional here that the girls grow up and marry and leave, and the boys stay and take over the ranch."

In addition to his responsibilities running their cattle ranch and guest ranch business, Tack is doing research for a book about the Van Cleve family. He has traced his heritage back to 1653 and Mad Duke John William of Cleves in the Netherlands. He estimated that twelve or thirteen generations have produced about 20,000 descendants of the mad duke living today.

Van Cleve also collects and restores antique cars and assorted other antiques. He pulled out a piano player—not a player piano—and hooked it up, and I watched in disbelief as little mechanical hammer "fingers" poked out and actually played a waltz.

Van Cleve has watched skeptically as Big Timber and the Boulder drainage have become popular places to live. "Hollywood is creeping in," he stated. "They move here to escape, then try to create the exact same thing they moved from. Why, when we get a blizzard we're content to wait for the county to plow as soon as they can get to it. But these newer residents call and hassle the road crew. They want instant service; they don't understand that you go with the flow here."

I have a soft spot for Big Timber. In January 1978 I was driving my push-button '62 Valiant along Highway 191, pulling a little one-wheeled trailer containing a few belongings. The ice and snow on the road was several inches thick. The tire blew out on the trailer, and I pulled over to figure out what to do. A storm was getting ready to unleash, the wind was howling, and dusk was rushing in.

Well, you can't jack up a one-wheeled trailer, and besides, I didn't have a spare. As I stood there mulling over the options, one rancher stopped, then another, and another. In just ten minutes we had heaved that little trailer into one of the pickups and set out for Big Timber. The fellow at the gas station didn't have a tire for it but said sure, leave it there as long as I needed. So off I went, right on time for my meeting and secure in the knowledge that all was well.

That trailer sat there until I could fetch it in springtime, and all the gas station fellow would take in payment was a handshake.

Big Timber has a number of studios, galleries, and shops. The Grand Hotel has been renovated into a classy, comfortable bed and breakfast hotel, and the dining room serves some of Montana's finest gourmet food. For dinner, servers carve the rack of lamb at your tableside, or present delicacies such as champagne shrimp, Key lime chicken, and filet mignon Béarnaise. The specials might include roasted duck with wild rice and chokecherry giblets, or smoked salmon with spinach fettuccine. Desserts are everything you'd expect of rich chocolate or fruit concoctions.

The restaurant is classic Montana and the menu is elegant. Black and white photographs by Tack's sister, Barbara Van Cleve, of rodeos and the West adorned the walls above white linen tablecloths. Patrons either were dressed nicely in "casual elegance" or came straight off the river from fishing. There wasn't a necktie in sight.

The stairs to the rooms had a wonderful creakiness. The rooms are furnished with antique bedroom sets and rugs. The baths are in a spotless central suite of showers, tubs, toilets, and sinks. The only concessions to modernity were the new mattresses—thank goodness.

Follow McLeod Street south out of downtown. In the park at the edge of town, a monument to the Sweet Grass Woolen Mill reminds residents that Montana was once the largest wool producer in the nation. The mill was situated along the Boulder River. Today, the interstate highway claims that site.

There still are some sheep raised around here. Several bands along the Boulder were guarded by shaggy white Great Pyrenees dogs who were not amused by me taking pictures of *their* sheep.

There are two Boulder Rivers in Montana, as well as numerous Boulder Creeks and Elk Creeks and Rock Creeks and Wolf Creeks and Clear Creeks and Deer Creeks and Muddy Creeks and Moose Creeks and Beaver Creeks. Early explorers were descriptive perhaps, but not big on originality. *This* Boulder River flows north out of the Absaroka Range and empties into the Yellowstone River near Big Timber. The other flows east and south from the Continental Divide near Butte, and empties into the Jefferson River near Whitehall.

The road crosses and recrosses the Boulder River, past pastures, hayfields, and splendid vistas of the Absaroka and Beartooth ranges. The views and peacefulness are wonderful. One pasture had at least a hundred grazing deer—I had to look twice to see if it was perhaps a deer farm. Nope.

It wouldn't be a complete trip without stopping at the McLeod Bar and Roadkill Cafe, where the motto is "From Your Grill To Ours." You have to have a sense of humor, of course.

Owners Bob and Claire Bryan thought up the name when they were sitting around the fire on a camping trip. They don't actually serve fried skunk or sautéed prairie dogs. Instead, they dish up great Eastern-style hoagies or spicy hot McLeod chicken wings. A display of photos in their Saloon of Dubious Decorum shows their Christmas and Halloween celebrations. You can leaf through a photo album while quaffing a brew from Australia, Mexico, Germany, or the Netherlands, and see pictures of their award-winning Bar of the Stars float for the Big Timber rodeo parade.

Property in this Boulder River area has been snapped up by a number of the rich and famous. Whoopi Goldberg, Michael Keaton, Tom Brokaw, Brooke Shields, Tom McGuane, Tom MacNamee, and Richard Wheeler all call this area home for some part of the year. And nearly all of them show up at the McLeod Bar sooner or later.

Livingston has a well-deserved reputation for wind. The wind blows so hard here, in fact, that the modern windmills on a power-generating wind farm blew right over.

Right: Abandoned Catholic Church at Ringling.
Below: McLeod Bar/Roadkill Cafe, where the motto is, "From Our Grill to Yours."

Claire Bryan takes it in stride. "It was on one long winter night last year," she related. "I was just ready to close, and a few cars pulled up. This familiar-looking guy came in with some others, and I thought maybe it was one of the summer people back already. After they all left I asked my husband if he knew who that was, and he said it was Robert Redford.

"Well heck, I didn't feel too bad," she said. "He didn't recognize me either."

A mile past the bar, the backroads route heads west on the West Boulder Road. A side trip south on the main Boulder River Road leads to a dead end, but what a dead end—surrounded by magnificent wilderness and mountains.

You'll hardly notice the slow pace and jostling surface of the West Boulder Road because your eyes will be glued to the surroundings. The Absaroka–Beartooth Wilderness rises to the south and the Crazy Mountains fill the northern horizon. It's riveting. The road eventually descends down the narrow Mission Creek canyon and ends as Swingley Road, just north of Livingston.

Livingston has a well-deserved reputation for wind. The wind blows so hard here, in fact, that the modern windmills on a power-generating wind farm blew right over.

Batten down your hat and ramble around downtown. The Livingston Depot Center has been beautifully restored and warrants a visit to see the architecture, as well as to view the art exhibits and historic displays. Park County Museum and Sleeping Giant Wildlife Museum also attract many visitors. The Livingston Bar & Grill serves fine meals.

In case you hadn't yet noticed, this is one of the few trips in Montana where you can gleefully eat your way around the area. The cluster of fine eating establishments is unique—take advantage of it. Fare on many of the other backroad stops is limited to fried pre-pressed burgers and iceberg lettuce salads with a token wedge of a tomato look-

alike—must be look-alikes 'cause they sure don't taste like tomatoes.

South of Livingston, travel Route 540 up the Paradise Valley to Chico Hot Springs. The open-air pools are wonderful, as are the comfortable accommodations. Chico has a multi-state reputation for excellent cuisine. You won't be disappointed. You can work off the meal later, dancing in the bar. They usually have live music on weekends. Or head south into Yellowstone National Park for some vigorous hiking or cross-country skiing.

Driving west from Pine Creek, Forest Road 6917 heads west over Trail Creek Pass and down Meadow Creek. It's mostly open ranchlands and the views extend over the surrounding mountain ranges: Gallatins, Hyalites, and Absarokas.

Jog east on the interstate to the next exit, and drive winding Jackson Creek Road west to Bridger Canyon. Once in the canyon, head north. (Just in case your gut isn't totally distended, pop into Bozeman to eat at the Bistro. It's your last chance for superb dining on this "eatathon" loop!)

The Silver Forest Inn is a lovely bed and breakfast lodge near Bridger Bowl Ski Area. Once an artists' retreat, this log inn offers an unforgettable view of sunrise on the Bridgers. I stayed in the upstairs turret room. Tucked cozily into bed, I could watch the constellations move across the sky through the big windows on three sides of the turret.

Bridger Bowl is known for abundant, light, powdery snow known as "cold smoke." You can see five mountain ranges from the top of the lift, and ski on over fifty runs, bowls, glades, trails, and slopes. Keep your eyes on the couloirs at the summit. You may see a few gonzo skiers shooting the chutes. Considering the almost vertical pitch, it's safe to say they don't ski the chutes. It's more like flying with a few brief touchdowns en route.

The paved road ends a few miles north of Bridger Bowl. Then it's twenty miles of bumpy road to Wilsall. The route of-

fers terrific views of the Bridger Range, then flows out of the foothills into the Shields River Valley. At that point it's a dilemma which way to look, east to the Crazies, or west back to the Bridgers. In the morning, the Bridgers are lit by golden sunrise colors; the Crazies reflect a rosy alpenglow at sunset.

For a break from continuous jolting in the vehicle, take a side trip up to Fairy Lake for a picnic and a walk in the Bridger Range. A foot path leads about two miles from the lake up Sacajawea Peak, two very steep miles, but splendid hiking. The trail leads through meadows of wildflowers, heather, and twisted windswept conifers. The summit has vertical exposures that may induce you to sit, rather than stand, but it requires no technical expertise. Just put one foot in front of the other and walk carefully to the top. It's worth it.

Silos in a dryland wheatfield in Meagher County.

47

10 Ruby River/Madison River

Guests sunned themselves and watched the town activity from the upper porch of the Fairweather Inn in Virginia City. The inn's floor had a wonderful, old-sounding creakiness. Our room was furnished in attractive old-style chintz and florals. The very proper sitting-room furniture was upholstered in velvet. The only anomaly was the new green garden hose coiled on the hallway wall-spigot—fire safety.

Virginia City and Nevada City are definitely tourist towns. But they do such a good job of it that you don't mind being the tourist. You can ride a train, a stagecoach, a wagon, or a horse while tour guides reel off facts and history in their spiels. It's a painless way to learn about the area. The restorations are authentic, shops and museums line the main streets, music trickles out of the saloons, and visitors just plain have a good time.

My sisters and I decided to get an old-time photo of ourselves as a keepsake. There were all sorts of costume choices: desperadoes, showgirls, cowgirls, schoolmarms, Indians, or whatever. Having been properly brought up by a minister, we didn't hesitate at all when selecting our outfits—floozies. It was as much fun getting dressed in petticoats and corsets and feathers as it was showing our families the photographs.

Every summer evening there is live entertainment. The Virginia City Players perform melodramas, followed by "A Varied Vigorous Vagary of Vivacious Variety Acts." It's fun to sit in the Old Stone Barn Theatre, watch the entertainment, and listen to the one-man-band cremona (theater organ) toot and whistle and bang out old tunes. The melodramas and humor made me glad I was born in this era, rather than subjugated to turn-of-the-century social norms.

On the other side of town, the Brewery Players have developed a much more spontaneous evening of gags, songs, slapstick, and tomfoolery. It's obvious they have as good a time as the audience. "We still haven't quite determined what happened last week," laughed ragtime pianist Ken Christensen.

"Midway through 'Itty Bitty Fishes' Mike forgot the words and he started ad libbing. I got laughing so hard the audience picked up on it and started laughing, until it brought the house down. I could barely play the last few measures because I was laughing so hard. And Mike just kept right on making up lyrics.

"It's one of the things I like best about cabaret," acknowledged Mike Verdon. "I never know what's going to pop out of my mouth next."

You can drink a beer or pop while watching the cabaret at the old H.S. Gilbert Brewery. They don't need sound amplification in this small theater, and a pleasantly casual atmosphere surrounds the professional performance. One actor dropped out of the ceiling onto the old brewing apparatus; the actresses shimmied around the audience and thoroughly embarrassed some delighted men; the jokes were funny and the songs melodic.

There are bats in the brewery, and leaks in the roof. When it rains hard it drips onto the stage and audience. "There have been a few performances when we could see our breath," stated Verdon. "But it's worth every minute."

Christensen is a trained classical pianist who teaches at Montana State University. But his greatest delight is playing right here. "This is where ragtime was meant to be played," he said. "Right here on an authentic instrument in this kind of setting. I love it."

When Christensen first started playing here years ago, the piano was severely out of tune. "The low end was very flat, and the high end was sharp," he said. "It sounded like one of those old music machines." Christensen trotted over to the piano and played a verse of the "Dill Pickles Rag," then ran through it again with each hand playing in a different key. "There. It sounded just like that!" he laughed.

Christensen and Verdon are hooked on Virginia City. "Honestly, you couldn't find more characters in any other square mile on earth," Christensen said.

"We get our best comedy material by just watching the locals interact with the tourists," added Verdon. "At the end of the season we do a show just for the local people. They drink and heckle, and we do take-offs on them and make it raunchy. Everybody has a great time. One local woman here talks like a truck driver and looks like Jack Nicholson with a sex change. She's always full of smiles and threats. Another manages a bar and mourns the old days. She says that ever since Flower Power the kids just don't get into the really good brawls anymore. Her husband was so bored here one winter he instigated a bad breath contest—and won. There's just no lack of great material right here in Virginia City."

Alder Gulch has held its share of treasure-seekers wanting a slice of the $100 million of gold mined here. You can pan for gold at River of Gold in Virginia City. West of town, near Alder, Steven Cox operates the Red Rock Mine, providing a modern-day answer for tourists in a hurry to discover their own quick treasures. He fills buckets with gravel from his property, then teaches you how to wash it away and find the Montana sapphires and garnets. He'll even polish and mount the gems in earrings or rings or whatever.

Alder is a "don't blink or you'll miss it" town. As in nearly all wide spots in the road, a few little human-made jewels are scattered about. The Oxbow Cafe has vinyl booths upholstered in Guernsey cow motif. Really. Vinyl Guernsey decor. Next door, Chick's Bar mixes locals and visitors around its horseshoe-shaped bar. The juke box selections reflect just how varied the customers are: Lynyrd Skynyrd, Favorite Polkas, the Beatles, Johnny Cash, All the Best From Ireland, Bryan Adams, Merle Haggard, Dr. Hook, Aretha Franklin, and Patsy Cline all share equal billing. Does the person who stocks this machine chuckle while filling the record slots?

When we were at Chick's everyone was feasting on free chili verde and rice. Some fellow from California vacations here every year, and shows his appreciation for the locals'

warmth and friendship by cooking one giant Mexican-style meal for everybody. Ready to share the bounty was a lady in hip waders, plaid flannel shirt, and bright pink cap advertising farm implements. Next in line, a fellow with a foot-long white beard sported suspenders under a Chick's Bar jacket. Behind him stood a slim farmer who had just finished irrigating. Following *him* stood a group of chattering students home from college, and last in line were a few tight-jeaned cowboys and their even-tighter-jeaned lady friends.

Want a slice of Montana? Stop in at Chick's Bar in Alder.

South of Alder, the route follows the Ruby River through an arid landscape of dry sage hills and sandstone bluffs. Gulches snake up off the river; moose and deer browse in the bottoms; the Snowcrest Range rises prominently to the south. Photographers will have a field day documenting the tumble-down buildings, glistening river, flashy wildflowers, wooden bridges, and canyon and mountain scenes.

One of those innocuous-looking gulches off Ruby Reservoir shelters a swatch of history from the earliest native peoples who inhabited Montana in the Paleolithic Era. When I worked in Barton Gulch the last week of June, the grass was so wet our shoes squished. People had to move their sleeping tents to higher ground. When the cold rain unleashed, everyone hunkered down in the big kitchen tent, reading or talking, grateful for rainsuits and wool and down and polypropylene. When the clouds let up, the crews sprang into action, getting in a few hours of work before the next deluge.

Volunteers have come to this archeological site for the past six summers. They're hooked on the excitement of discovering what human life may have been like 9,400 years ago. It takes a rare person to leap for joy at finding bone fragments or carbonized seeds, but these folks do.

The Barton Gulch site is significant for many reasons. It provides the first evidence that Paleoindians ate plant foods. To me, it seemed perfectly logical that our ancestors ate berries

There were all sorts of costume choices: desperadoes, showgirls, cowgirls, schoolmarms, Indians, or whatever. Having been properly brought up by a minister, we didn't hesitate at all when selecting our outfits—floozies.

South of Alder, the route follows the Ruby River through an arid landscape of dry sage hills and sandstone bluffs. Gulches snake up off the river; moose and deer browse in the bottoms; the Snowcrest Range rises prominently to the south. Photographers will have a field day documenting the tumble-down buildings, glistening river, flashy wildflowers, wooden bridges, and canyon and mountain scenes.

Trumpeter swan in Red Rock Lakes National Wildlife Refuge.

BRUCE SELYEM

and seeds and greens, as well as deer and rabbits and bison, but this site offers the proof. Until now, research concentrated on the big kill sites, such as buffalo jumps. Earlier evidence had indicated that Paleoindians subsisted entirely by hunting for red meat. But Barton Gulch has unique "paleokitchens" where tools, cooking pits, and plant remains demonstrate otherwise. There are even objects that may have been toys for children.

People of the Hearth: Paleoindians of the Northern Rockies is a video documenting this archeology dig sponsored by the Museum of the Rockies. It speculatively demonstrates the uses of various tools and kitchen set-ups. Sound dry? It isn't. Look for it at the museum in Bozeman. The video shows people scraping hides with sharpened stone tools, cooking in leaf-lined pits, chipping obsidian into razor-sharp arrowheads, and using an atlatl, the Paleoindian's dart-throwing stick.

I got to play with the atlatl. It was amazing to feel the powerful thrust you could muster. When everything went right, and I threw that dart straight and true at the target, it felt like hitting the sweet spot on a tennis racket or golf club—pure physical joy.

As you drive along the Ruby Reservoir, glance around at the adjacent hills and gulches, and imagine a Paleoindian village, smoke curling up from roasting pits, and children shouting and playing. It gives a whole different perspective to the region.

The route climbs between the Snowcrest and Gravelly ranges, then drops into the Centennial Valley. The wildlife-viewing in this valley always astonishes me. In the course of one afternoon we watched a trumpeter swan family glide across Lower Red Rock Lake; saw a coyote pounce on a mouse; held our breath as a goshawk dove at a red fox and swerved aside at the last moment; laughed at pronghorn antelope bounding along; and wondered about two dozen ravens lined up in a row, each perched on a fence-post, facing into the wind.

You need weeks, not hours, to really appreciate Red Rock Lakes National Wildlife Refuge and the Centennial Valley and Mountains. Besides the abundant mammal population, 261 species of birds have been sighted in this area. Most are migratory, so you'll see different species during each season of the year.

All roads into Red Rocks are closed by snow in winter, and are largely impassable after a hard summer rainstorm. If the weather and season are right, take a canoe, hiking boots, binoculars, spotting scope, field guides to animals and birds and flowers, camera, mosquito repellent, and clothes to deal

Top: A fishin' aficionado.
Above: A trip east on Highway 287 leads through the narrow Madison River Canyon to Quake Lake and the site of the landslide of 1959.

with extreme weather variations. Winter visitors have to ski or snowmobile to get there.

East of the Centennial Valley, Highway 87 climbs over Raynolds Pass from Idaho and drops into the Madison River Valley in Montana. The Madison Range is riveting, with alpine meadows and snowy couloirs atop 11,000-foot peaks.

The Madison River originates in nearby Yellowstone National Park. A side trip east on Highway 287 leads through the narrow Madison River Canyon to Quake Lake and the site of the big landslide of 1959. In a mere eight seconds, 80 million tons of rocks loosened by an earthquake rocketed 1,200 feet to the valley below and climbed partway up the other side, damming the river, burying campgrounds, and destroying the road. The 175-m.p.h. winds created by the falling mountain tossed two-ton automobiles around like they were confetti.

The earthquake rocked Hebgen Lake waters into gigantic seiches, or standing waves, much as children playing in their bath water create a sloshing, jostling mass of waves. This quaking play of nature sent twenty-foot-high waves down Hebgen Lake that cracked, but did not wash out, the dam.

The Visitor Center is built atop the landslide rubble. From the Center, you can see the raw cut of yellow soil where the slide occurred, find sections of the old highway askew, and view before-and-after photos. From the highway between Quake and Hebgen lakes, look north for the fifteen-foot-high scarp, or cliff, at the base of the mountains. It is a very visible earthquake fault, showing where the river valley dropped and the mountain range rose during the earthquake. It's a sobering reminder of just how puny we humans are.

Highway 287 travels north along the Madison River, and climbs atop old river terraces for views of this broad valley ringed by mountains. Meadowlarks sing from fenceposts and rocks, deer and cattle and pronghorn graze in the same pastures, and the noteworthy outline of Sphinx Peak dominates the eastern horizon.

The Madison is a well-known blue-ribbon trout fishery, probably the most popular fishing river in Montana. Anglers float in canoes, rafts, and drift-boats. Some bob along in those float tubes that always remind me of day-old goslings wobbling around on a current.

The riverbanks are dotted with coolers and jackets and fishing paraphernalia. Spouses lounge in lawn chairs while the other halves creep through the grass to deep pools, or wade in the shallow riffles. Moose, mink, beaver and waterbirds all cruise these waters and banks, sharing the shore with people and cattle and horses.

Ennis is your basic fly-fishing mecca. Parked in front of the various fly shops, outfitter headquarters, and motels are license plates from all over the country sporting motifs like LIV2FISH, ANGLER, GOFISH, TROUT, FLYFISH, and WANNAFISH.

Adding another carat to the gem-like fishing and outdoor opportunities around here, the small Continental Divide restaurant provides gourmet dinners. People just off the river in flannel shirts or shorts and T-shirts dine next to those who dressed up for an evening out. Typical Montana. Diners select from the menu or the server's recitation of the evening specialties, such as fresh seared salmon with raspberry sauce, spicy barbecued shrimp New Orleans, veal chops with shiitake mushrooms, and other French-Italian-American bistro sorts of culinary delights. It's always worth stopping for dinner here. In fact, it's worth a special trip to Ennis just to dine at the Continental Divide.

After dinner, those wanting a lively evening should drive just south of Ennis to the Blue Moon Saloon. I, however, drove north to Norris Hot Springs. If you ignore the ornery owner, this funky hole-in-the-pasture pool is a real delight. You can float under the big sky and get about as mellow as a human can be without actually melting into a puddle.

11 Tendoy Mountains– Grasshopper Creek

Yesterday's Calf-A is not just another roadside eatery—it's an encounter. Your first clue is its name. Second clue, the boneyard of old implements and oddities and antlers you must navigate to reach the front door of this old schoolhouse. Inside the door, the sign reads: "Dell is 6,007 feet above sea level. Watch your step."

The cafe serves decent meals, at the counter or family-style at long wooden tables. The menu is written on a blackboard. Shelves line the walls, crammed with photos, antiques, rocks and minerals, knickknacks, and books with titles like *Practical Farming* (1937); *Making Sure of Arithmetic*, and the *Elson Grammar School Reader* (1911).

Pies are homemade, patrons watch the cook prepare each meal behind the counter, and visitors share conversations at the long tables. A nearby shed is chock-a-block full of historic paraphernalia, open for your browsing pleasure.

Dell is so-named because it sits in one. As in, the Farmer in the Dell. Or, more appropriately in this case, the rancher in the dell. This secluded little Red Rock River valley runs along the base of the Tendoy Mountains. Dell originated as a stop for the Union Pacific Railroad. Today it's a stop for interstate travelers.

The Dell Mercantile has a few of a lot of things: gas, groceries, caps, fishing tackle, and other southwest Montana essentials. The hotel/bar/cafe provides very basic lodgings upstairs: $15 for a single, $20 for a double. Thin wood-paneled walls ensure you'll need no alarm clock; assorted fishing and hunting guests stomp off to kill things in the early morning hours.

West of Dell, Big Sheep Creek cuts an opening through the Tendoy Mountains. Follow the Back Country Byway signs to stay on the route. This is very rocky, dry, steep country, with sagebrush and juniper clinging to the arid slopes. With names like Deadman's Creek, Pileup Canyon, Tonsilitis Gulch, Four Eyes Canyon, and Alkali Creek, you'll expect to see a character out of a Zane Grey novel come riding pell-mell over some ridge, chased by the bad guys.

Anglers fished the creek for rainbows, browns, and cutthroats, and ranchers moved cattle along the road to higher pastures. We watched a few bighorn sheep settle in for an afternoon siesta on a scree slope. They pawed the rocks into some semblance of level, lowered their forequarters then hindquarters, and suddenly disappeared in perfect camouflage. With a look through the binoculars, we realized the larger boulders on the slope were actually other resting bighorns. The band of 25 included ewes, rams, and lambs, all soaking up the afternoon warmth.

Swallows had built their condominiums on the cliffs over the creek, and were feasting on the abundant (and annoying) insect life while giving us a spectacular display of aerial acrobatics. The trout were quite visible in the clear water of the stream.

The Tendoys display fascinating geology along the road. Convoluted, twisted rocks show the folding and faulting and warping of these Paleozoic and Mesozoic formations. Hoodoos, sheer cliffs, arches, and window rocks decorate the limestone walls.

The road emerges quite suddenly into a big, open valley permeated with the sharp smells of hot sage and rabbitbrush. The rust-orange talus slopes of the Beaverhead Range dominate the western skyline. A few trees grow in the drainages below the stark relief of the rocky summits.

I walked quietly over a slight rise and sat down beside a large sagebrush just as a band of pronghorns caught sight of me. They started to flee, but curiosity won. They walked closer, sniffing and whistling, with lots of sudden bolting away, until the whole band was within 25 feet of me. Then I enjoyed a remarkable sight: they began circling, one after another, until I was the center pole of a living merry-go-round. They went from a trot into that unique springing pogo-stick bound that's best described as a *sproing*. Round and round, closer and closer to

Above: *Pronghorn antelope stops to look before* sproing*ing away.*
Right: *History comes alive during Bannack Days, the third weekend of July.*

about ten feet away, until the leader, inquisitiveness apparently satisfied, *sproing*ed out of the circle and led the bouncing band over the hill.

Parts of this road looked suspiciously like a two-track through the fields. You'll open and close gates, chase cattle out of the way, and travel very, very slowly. Most stretches were well-graded, other sections had deep ruts from the last storm.

Island Butte sits out in that big valley, forcing the road to detour around it. A cow moose and her calf were way out in the sagebrush near the butte. They spooked at the sight of the car, and started running toward Simpson Creek a mile away. The mother trotted briskly and hurtled fences en route, the gawky

calf scrambled around the bushes and squirmed through the fences. It caught a hind leg in the wires, and I cringed at possibly causing a broken leg. Fortunately the calf struggled free and scurried along again, following its mother across the road and disappearing into the willows along the creek.

The road crosses a small ridge above Medicine Lodge Creek. In the 1860s, freighter teams followed this route to bring supplies from Corrine, Utah, to the gold camp at Bannack. Today, a powerline descends the pass in straight lines, while the road snakes down that same hill with considerable wavering and weaving.

Medicine Lodge Creek runs through a long narrow valley

Left: *Meade Hotel, Bannack.*
Above: *Yesterday's Calf–A restaurant and museum (eats and oddities, and fun).*

The Tendoys display fascinating geology along the road. Convoluted, twisted rocks show the folding and faulting and warping of these Paleozoic and Mesozoic formations. Hoodoos, sheer cliffs, arches, and window rocks decorate the limestone walls.

dotted with ranches, and eventually empties into Clark Canyon Reservoir. The road meanders alongside the creek to its junction with Highway 324, near Grant.

Graeme and Bev McDougall live in Grant because of the relaxed lifestyle. "We don't have to put up with anyone, or keep up with the Joneses, or anything," Graeme chuckled, "because here everybody has a low standard of living.

"The big excitement is the school Christmas play. Really, in Grant nobody puts on any airs. You are what you are. Take it or leave it. We have our ex-felon, our resident alcoholic, the illicit drug user, and all the so-called normal ones. People are pretty tolerant, in reality. Of course they complain about each other a lot..."

McDougall epitomizes the term "laid-back." Laconic and relaxed, he talked about his Last Best Place outfitting business, and running traplines with his dogsled team. "My snowmobile quit one time too many, and I had to walk sixteen miles out. So I got these dogs," he said. "The only problem I ever had was right at first, and I learned real quick to tie 'em up tight while I check the traps, or else they'll be waiting for me back home, grinnin' and happy to see me walk in."

When the outfitting business stops for the winter, McDougall builds custom graphite and bamboo fishing rods. Six boxes of tinsel and feathers and fluff attested to his fly-tying sideline.

"I like autumn here the best," he stated. "Carrying a rifle is a great excuse to go walk around for a few weeks. My step into insanity is rock-climbing. I started on a dare, and now I love the mental challenge of it."

McDougall belongs to the local Search & Rescue team. Four years ago the team went to rescue a climber who had fallen off a mountain, and they realized no one had the expertise to lead a technical climb to retrieve her. McDougall took lessons and now climbs for Search & Rescue as well as just for fun.

Ten miles west of Grant, a Forest Service road follows the Lewis and Clark Trail up Lemhi Pass. Ascending the pass, we saw moose, deer, elk, and rabbits. The pass affords a good view east down lovely Horse Prairie Valley, and west into Idaho's Lemhi Valley and Mountains. You can drive several miles north on Warmsprings Road to see bigger views into Idaho.

Interpretive signs on the pass and at the campground commemorate Lewis and Clark and their Indian guide Sacajawea. They reached this point August 12, 1805. Lewis wrote of elation when, "The road took us to the most distant fountain of the waters of the Mighty Missouri in surch of which we have spent so many toilsome days and wristless nights." And he wrote of disappointment at seeing the massive mountains still ahead, wishing to be "taisting the waters of the great Columbia this evening."

Twelve miles north of Grant, a state park preserves Bannack, the gold-rush cradle of Montana. The interpretive signs are informative, but the signmakers should have hired a grammarian before posting them.

You can stroll the boardwalk and walk through the hotel, schoolhouse, and homes. The Visitor Center provides plenty of background information to enhance your tour. Rowdy prisoners were chained to the rings in the jailhouse floor; Methodist minister William Van Orsdel, Brother Van, nudged the populace into building Montana Territory's first church; the gallows marked the end of Sheriff Henry Plummer and his thieving band of road agents.

Miners pulled gold out of Grasshopper Creek and environs in a multitude of ways. From the early rockers and sluices, through hydraulic water jets, and on to underground hard rock tunneling, the area produced nearly $40 million of gold in just its first five years.

The gold panned out, and Bannack was basically abandoned by the 1930s. But the lure of gold still has a hold on our populace—miners today continue to search the region for that elusive precious metal.

12 Big Hole River– Pioneer Mountains

The Pioneer Mountains are split into two distinct ranges, east and west. The East Pioneers tend to be more rugged and remote, with alpine meadows, wilderness, and lakes reflecting 11,000-foot summits. The West Pioneers are lower, more rounded, and riddled with roads and timber cuts.

Grasshopper Creek—the very same Grasshopper Creek of gold-rush fame around Bannack—originates in the Pioneers and flows south between the two ranges. Wise River runs north between the mountains. The Wise River–Polaris road parallels the two waterways and provides multiple access points into both ranges. This picturesque route is designated a National Forest Scenic Byway.

South to north, a profusion of cabins and vacation homes divides the once-pastoral valley. But development was probably inevitable, with good hunting, fishing, hiking, camping, downhill skiing and natural hot springs in the vicinity.

Maverick Mountain is a modest homestyle ski area, great for families and those of us who don't care to invest in fancy ski outfits. The snow is pretty reliable and the views are beautiful.

Elkhorn Hot Springs is once again worth a visit. It has endured considerable neglect over the past decade, but the new owners are putting their hearts and wallets into rejuvenating it. The meals are plain and tasty, the cabins and rooms clean, the green slime was banished from the outdoor pools, and the indoor hot tub/steam is a toasty 110 degrees. There are horses to ride, trails to walk, a creek to fish, and simple relaxation to be found here.

A talkative cowboy from Fort Peck was doing handyman work around the place. He told stories and jokes while he fixed pipes and lighting in the bathhouse, then continued entertaining us the next morning over coffee.

Driving up the road, we slowed to watch a blue heeler herding three mules along the road. The dog urged the mules into a trot, ran back to the truck in front of us (for further instructions?), then raced ahead and turned the mules onto a side road. The truck driver never once got out in the several miles we followed. Presumably he had done all his work previously by training the dog so well.

Crystal Park is a unique geological attraction atop the Wise River–Grasshopper Creek divide. A summertime volunteer from the Butte Gem and Mineral Club aids rockhounds and curious tourists who dig for quartz, amethyst and limonite crystals.

My sisters and I strolled around the crystal-digging area. A pair of fellows were knee deep in a hole, one shoveling dirt, and the other shaking dirt through a sifter. They had just met that morning and decided it would be more fun to work together. "That way at least we'll get good stories, even we don't find no good crystals," grinned the big retired Idahoan.

The skinny one from Missoula was on vacation. He loves digging the crystals, and his wife makes necklaces to give as Christmas presents. He handed me a small crystal to keep, saying they hadn't found much yet "but we're hopin'. That's the fun of it."

We wandered farther, discovering what could be the origin for the term mine field. This area was completely riddled by the craters and hollows and pits dug by enthusiastic crystal-seekers. The roots of a few struggling trees were exposed down several feet by the excavations, and the ground was denuded of its grassy cover. It looked remarkably like photos from a war—except here the people in the trenches wore shorts instead of fatigues and carried shovels instead of rifles.

I stopped to watch a family of diggers from Hamilton. The father was about five feet down a hole, working intently, and never even looked up. The mother and two youngsters dug in a big open pit. The children were having an absolute ball getting filthy and looking for treasure. It was indeed a great way to spend a Sunday afternoon with the family.

I moseyed on down the trail to find my sisters, who had

TOM DIETRICH

Above: *Beaverslide haystacker near Wisdom.*

Facing page: *Wise River offers fishing, hiking, and critter-watching.*

presumably gone ahead to the car. No sign of them there, so I climbed back up the hill to find them squatting in a cavity, skirts and all, and—surprise—digging for crystals. They had found some pretty specimens and were not a bit interested in leaving just then, so, if you can't beat 'em...

The ghost town of Coolidge is a few miles east of the main road. The tumble-down buildings and old mine are quite photogenic, and children will revel in the sight of the creek burbling through a classroom of the old schoolhouse.

The road down the Wise River drainage has as many turns and meanders as a slow stream. Views are extensive, wildflowers colorfully abundant, and wildlife watching is excellent. The region nourishes moose, elk, mule deer, black bears, bighorn sheep, and mountain goats, as well as bald eagles and other raptors.

Get out of the car and take a hike on one of the many trails, drop a line into one of the feeder streams, watch the beavers working their ponds, or spread out a picnic and listen to a meadowlark serenade. This is prime recreation territory. Take advantage of it.

The one-horse town of Wise River caters to recreationists, specifically anglers. Apply a liberal coating of mosquito repellent, and go out for some of Montana's most famous fishing in the Big Hole River. The Anaconda–Pintlers rise to the north; wild baby's breath and gooseberries and mint grow on the riverbanks; horses graze in the nearby fields; frisky trout present a challenge.

Ralph Nichols has ranched on the Big Hole River for 42 years. In addition to ranching, he's a paleontologist and research assistant for Carnegie Museum of Natural History and for Idaho State University. Nichols published one of the first vertebrate paleontology studies of the Lemhi Valley in Idaho, and recently he donated several thousand specimens to the university. His collection included three-toed horses, camels, rhinoceroses, antelope, and small animals, including a nearly complete skeleton of a tiny pocket gopher from 20 million years ago.

Nichols went to school in Missoula every winter quarter for eight years to get his master's degree in vertebrate paleontology. He's just a dissertation away from a doctorate now, and said he simply enjoys the challenge. He has worked the past three summers on a dig south of Salmon, Idaho—between calving, lambing, haying, and ranching full-time, as well as serving on the local school board.

Ralph and his wife Gayle like to take their daughters skiing at Lost Trail, or ride up into the hills and fish. "I've only fished the Big Hole once or twice in forty years," he said. "I'd rather get away a bit farther."

Sara, age nine, said her favorite part of ranch life is raising the bunnies and ducks and cats and dogs and horses. And chasing the coyotes away from the lambs. Juliette, Noodles, Root Beer and Shakes Beer all waddled behind us, then ran away quacking, as we walked around the barns. The ranch was built in 1908, and the log barns and home are simply beautiful.

"Sara here saved my life a few years ago," Nichols said. "We were riding the boundary fence up canyon, and the colt bucked me off. I bunged up my shoulder and punctured a lung and couldn't move. Nobody knew where we were. She rode back, opened gates and everything as tiny as she was, and got help."

The Nicholses raise crossbred cattle: Angus, Charolais and Hereford. They winter their cattle down at a friend's ranch near Divide, and take the friend's cattle each summer on the Nichols ranch. The arrangement has worked for 42 years.

The Nicholses also raise saddle horses and bulls, and a few sheep.

"Just a few sheep now," Ralph laughed. "We bought our first band from a shoestring outfit held together with rope and a few boards. We had a dickens of a time getting them loaded, then stopped in Anaconda on the way home. Gayle ran in for groceries; the ewes were bawling and blatting and the lambs were crying. It sounded like we were killing them. It was so embarrassing I scooched down in the seat and the girls wore Groucho Marx noses and glasses.

"We were totally unprepared for the first year of lambing. There were lambs everywhere. We kept building pens and adding on and finally even put some of 'em in the horse trailer. Those little guys could get out and be in the garden and on the lawn and everywhere. It was quite an experience."

The Nicholses have lost a lot of lambs to coyotes. "We got a guard dog, and worked her and trained her and did everything right, but she hated the sheep and wouldn't stay with them," Nichols said. "It was the darnedest thing. So now we just keep the sheep closer to the house, and that seems to help."

Nichols doesn't think the Big Hole area has changed much. "Cattle ranchers don't make much money," he stated. "Outsiders come and stay a while but then leave. Winters can get down to forty or fifty below, so you spend the whole summer preparing for winter and then your summer is gone. If you

have kids it's hard, too. There's only one other family with school-age children between here and Wisdom, so we have to shuttle the girls seventeen miles to school every day, and pick them up afterwards. You just have to like the life for it to be worth it. It is to us."

Wisdom is situated in the Big Hole Valley. Surely this is where the river was named, here where the huge open valley is clearly the highest and widest "hole" in western Montana. Hole was the mountain-man word for a valley surrounded by mountains.

Lewis and Clark originally named this river the Wisdom River, and nearby rivers the Philanthropy and the Philosophy. But early settlers were apparently not so high-minded, and renamed them the Big Hole, the Ruby, and the Beaverhead.

A major forest fire in Idaho sent dense smoke into the valley, which nearly occluded the August sun. The haze bestowed a specter-like aspect on the region: the tops of big haystacks appeared to float, detached from the base of the stack; the Bitterroot Mountains vanished and reappeared; vehicle headlights cast a peculiar sheen.

We stopped to rest and rub the smoke from our eyes in Wisdom. There, the Pioneer Mountain Restaurant served us the best apple-huckleberry crisp I've ever had the good fortune to eat. Next door, the Wisdom River Gallery displayed Western art and crafts. It was a very pleasant stop.

Just down the road, Sheila Kirkpatrick custom-makes cowboy hats at Kirkpatrick Hatters. There are only thirty or forty hatters in the United States, and in 1992 she was the first woman hatter inducted into the National Cowboy Hall of Fame.

"I was a hatter in Billings, then I married this cowboy and moved here and thought, 'Yea! I'm done working'," she said. "Ha! Word spread, and now I work six days a week. These hats go to people all over the U.S. and even to Europe and

Australia." In addition to making hats for working ranchers, she has hatted Cheryl Ladd, Hank Williams, Jr., and other actors and musicians.

Kirkpatrick designs each hat to flatter the wearer. A local Nez Perce woman makes beautiful beaded bands and brims for Kirkpatrick's "Lady Montana" hats.

"There are so many different crown styles and brim shapes and sizes," she said. "You have to consider each person's face, the size of their shoulders, the jawline, and colors. All of those are factors in whether a hat looks and feels right."

We watched her steam and mold a hat, then she added her special touch by lighting it on fire and sanding it to a finish as smooth and soft as a baby's bottom. After that, she put natural oils back in, for water repellency and longevity.

Kirkpatrick loves Wisdom. "There's every entertainment here you need," she stated. "There's horseshoe tournaments and street dances, and the county fair in Dillon every summer. That's plenty for us."

The Big Hole Valley grows notoriously good hay. I stopped at the Lapham Ranch near Jackson, where haying was in full swing. Debbie was in the house, baking bread and preparing the three meals a day she serves the haying crew. Their crew is consistent from year to year, comprised of teachers, relatives, and some high school and college students.

Many of the ranchers still stack hay with a beaverslide, which makes those distinctive, gigantic bread-loaf shaped haystacks that dot the valley for mile after mile. A beaverslide is a remarkably efficient, inexpensive log and lumber contraption developed in the nearby Beaverhead Valley.

Seventy-seven-year-old Bud Lapham was in charge of stacking, and his son Max oversaw the mowing. Hired hand Jackie Boetticher ran the wheeled rake, combing the loose-cut hay into even rows. I rode the buckrake with her husband Jimmy, racing along each row, scooping until you had to stand to see over the pile. After depositing each load at the base of the beaverslide, Bud started the tines, which lifted the load and flipped it onto the growing stack.

The Laphams make between four and seven big stacks a day. They grow enough hay for about 70 haystacks each year, so haying is intense for two to three weeks. The weather had been kind so far that summer, and no rain fell on the curing hay.

A beaverslide-stacked haystack averages about twenty tons. A single cow eats 20 to 25 pounds of hay a day (and drinks 10 to 12 gallons of water). At that rate, five hundred cows eat an entire stack in just under four days, which makes all those big stacks seem a bit smaller.

Jackson Hot Springs Lodge is the unofficial community center for the small town of Jackson. The warm pools are pleasant and clean, the lodgings comfortable, the meals fine, and the lodge is big enough for a great dance and party on such occasions as Old Timer's Day, New Year's Eve, or the Fireman's Ball.

Teresa Murdoch said there are trade-offs to living in such a small town. "You have fewer people to choose from for friendships," she admitted. "But that makes you learn to get along with whoever is there."

She teaches about ten children in her combined fifth through eighth grade classroom. "They become more individualized learners in this situation," she stated. "The older ones help the younger ones. A fifth grader sees the eighth grade math on the board and begins to understand even a little of it, and the eighth graders hear the younger grades' lessons repeated so they remember it better."

Teresa's husband Ken runs Broken Horn Outfitters, shoes horses, and does seasonal work for local ranchers. In addition to regular outfitting for hunters and anglers, he's trying to promote backcountry trips for the handicapped—from those missing an arm to quadriplegics. "They are the best people I've ever guided," he stated. "They're willing to go the extra mile where others take things for granted."

Ken spoke fondly of his horses, and his joy of being in the backcountry. "I was in the Gallatins and a blizzard hit. Hit hard," he recalled. "You couldn't see two inches in front of your face, and the sleet was soaking me to the skin. There was no place to stop where we were, and you couldn't ride the horse because a branch would sweep you off or poke your eyes out. So I got off, held my horse's tail and told him to go home. I followed that animal in absolute blinding conditions for eight miles. I couldn't even see the horse—just held his tail. When he stopped, we were right at the horse trailer."

The drive west to Big Hole Battlefield National Monument and Chief Joseph Pass is simply beautiful. The route crosses the open valley and enters rolling timbered hills. Low log fences zigzag along the roadside, without question the most attractive fencing I've ever seen. The scenic beauty is a good counterpoint to the distressing facts of the battlefield.

Otis Halfmoon is a park ranger at the battlefield. He is also a Nez Perce whose great-grandfathers were killed here in 1877. "I have such different emotions here," he said. "I've cried both for my people and for the white soldiers. They were all caught in the politics of the day. My people were just trying to find a home where they could live in peace. Many of the white soldiers were immigrants who could barely speak English. Some of them tried to help the Indian women and children get away from the murdering soldiers."

Halfmoon first came here as a child, with his parents. "They brought us here, and took us to the Bearpaws, to Yellowstone, to places in Idaho, and told us the stories," he said. "It's very important to know your history. They told us origin and coyote stories, about old-time religious beliefs. My mother taught us that the Creator made everything, the sun and earth and people and animals, and that everything has a spirit, that we are all one people. As a park ranger here I can present both sides of the story. That's very important."

"This tragedy here in this valley was a terrible thing, pitting brother against brother. Our skin may be different, our languages different. But beneath we are all one family. We will all die someday, and return to Mother Earth. We are one people. Never forget that."

BEVERLY R. MAGLEY

KENT & CHARLENE KRONE

DAVID A. WHITE

Above: *Big Hole Battlefield and Visitors' Center.*

Facing page, top left: *Sheila Kirkpatrick, custom hatter.*
Bottom left: *Quartz from Crystal Park digging area north of Polaris.*
Right: *A good place to tell fish stories.*

Halfmoon was raised on politics and negotiation. His father was on the tribal council for 33 years, and chairman for half of those years. As a park ranger, Otis Halfmoon reaches out to numerous communities of people, giving presentations and talks all around the region, and helping to coordinate Native American participation in the battlefield observances.

Halfmoon said he was a child of the '60s, with ribbon-wrapped braids to his waist, eagle feathers, love beads, and protest marches. "I knew my history very well," he stated. "I could knowledgeably be mad at Christianity, lies, and government policies. But that really hurt my mother and father. Dad is a war veteran, and kept reminding me that Indians have al-

ways enlisted in high numbers to fight for the United States. Now I know anger is not the answer."

I sat out on the deck at the battlefield that hot, sunny afternoon. On his day off, Halfmoon was giving an impromptu presentation to a large group there. I listened to him and watched the faces—people were alternately laughing, sad, and serious, and completely intent on the words of this excellent speaker. He ended with a point we must all take to heart: "This tragedy here in this valley was a terrible thing, pitting brother against brother. Our skin may be different, our languages different. But beneath we are all one family. We will all die someday, and return to Mother Earth. We are one people. Never forget that."

Spotted knapweed, Russian knapweed, diffuse knapweed—all members of the sunflower family, genus *Centaurea*. The name centaurea probably refers to a Greek centaur, or spearman, since the bracts around the flower heads are often spiny.

In its native habitat in Eurasia, knapweed is simply one of many wild flowers that have evolved a balance with other plant species. In Montana, however, knapweed has found ideal living conditions, no natural enemies, and virtually unlimited opportunities to procreate freely. So it does.

Each plant can produce up to 1,000 seeds. Knapweed leaves produce a chemical that gets into the ground and suppresses germination and growth of other plant species. Honey bees love the nectar and readily pollinate the blossoms. Consequently, knapweed is successfully wiping out native vegetation and invading Montana.

This is no benign invasion. The annual loss of forage plants to knapweed is estimated to be $4.5 million. It is in every county in the state, and researchers estimate that knapweed already covers 2 million acres of Montana. Fully one half of the entire state has growing conditions suitable for knapweed infestation.

It has spread because of human activity. We drive vehicles through the fields, pick up seeds in the tires and carry them elsewhere. We bundle knapweed up in bales of hay and ship it. The seeds stick in boot soles, or to hoofs, then we ride the horses and move the cows from fields to forests. Most grazing animals won't eat it.

The solution? Counties, ranchers, and farmers try to control it with herbicides. Researchers have released a fly that attacks the flower buds. Sheep will eat it. But it continues to spread.

What can you do? Pull it. Yank the sucker right out of the ground. If it is already going to seed, seal it in heavy plastic bags and dispose of it. Avoid driving off-road. Report infestations to the county weed control office.

Every year I take a five-day backpack trip with women friends. Last year we found an isolated patch of knapweed in the Bob Marshall Wilderness. None of us could stand it, so we spent an hour pulling the plants, wrapped and tied the 15-pound "bales" to our packs, and staggered out to our vehicles. It was worth every step.

I've watched it spread along the forest road where I walk daily. I make it a practice to pull two plants each walk. If we all yanked just one or two plants every day we could reduce and eventually eradicate knapweed from the state.

If China could eliminate flies from an entire nation, Montanans should be able to eliminate knapweed. Do your part. When you see it, yank it. And tell your neighbors.

13 Lost Trail Pass/Skalkaho Pass

The Lost Trail Pass area is winter wonderland, offering excellent alpine and nordic skiing. Nordic skiers can choose from numerous trails, reserve a Forest Service cabin and ski in for a cozy winter night by the fire. Alpine skiers ride efficient lifts and endure waiting lines about as long as your little finger. And everybody, pink-cheeked from the nippy air, meets in the hot pools at the bottom of the pass. Lost Trail Hot Springs has clean pools, and good accommodations and food. Other hot springs are scattered through the Bitterroot Valley.

The best dining and accommodations in this corner of the state are at the Broad Axe Lodge, near Sula. Guests can stay in immaculate cabins in a big open meadow along the East Fork of the Bitterroot River. The area is known for bighorn sheep, and diners often have binoculars next to their bread plates. The lodge's owners are personable and welcoming, and serve delicious dinners.

I didn't see bighorns through the picture windows, but the summer mountain scene, the hummingbirds at the window feeders, and the lawn-grazing bunnies kept me entertained. After dinner, I walked along the road, rounded a bend and saw a bighorn ewe and lamb drinking from the stream. They were skittish, but not particularly afraid, so I sat down in the trees and watched for about fifteen minutes. The lamb wanted a drink, but was afraid of the fast water. It was a quandary, and the ewe waited patiently until the lamb finally tiptoed close enough for a few gulps. Then they scrambled up into the woods, and I went on my way—every one of us, presumably, quite satisfied.

The monumental granite peaks of this section of the Bitterroot Range indicate the eastern limit of the Idaho Batholith. An enormous, mountain-carrying block of sedimentary rock slid off the top of that granite, and came to rest east of the Bitterroots. Those mountains are the Sapphires. The Bitterroot River carved a canyon between the two ranges, then 50 million years ago a volcano erupted and filled the south end of the Bitterroot Valley. That volcanic rock is called rhyolite—the gold-colored rock exposed in the bluffs along the river.

A roadside historic marker on Highway 93 tells of the Medicine Tree, in which a ram's horn is imbedded. Look beyond the tree to see human-looking profiles outlined in the rocks.

The Bitterroot is increasingly a bedroom community. The fertile valley fields sprout subdivisions alongside the orchards, farms, grainfields, dairies, and pastures. Property values have soared, and fancy new landscaped homes are adjacent to unkempt, run-down shacks and trailer houses. Retirees, medical researchers, loggers, survivalists, farmers, and religious fundamentalists all share the valley. Small businesses abound. Rubber-clad anglers speckle the length of the river, fishing for trout and largemouth bass. Four-wheel-drive vehicles are the norm. The knapweed infestation is appalling and alarming.

In 1825 a trader for the Hudson Bay Company named this "The Valley of Troubles." The name is still apropos. Trader Alexander Ross was frustrated at not being able to cross through deep snow to the Big Hole, and he became an unwilling resident for a time. Many of today's residents are frustrated but willing residents, embroiled in a major controversy over timber.

Logging is a big part of Darby's history and identity. But cutting trees isn't as straightforward as it once may have been. Residents feel the pinch of change as the public challenges rampant cutting of national forests. Private lands have been nearly cut clear of their forests, and timber workers fear for their livelihoods.

The issue has divided neighborhoods and families, and gets downright ugly at times. It is humanity at its worst, with the most rabid people finding outlet in destroying property and threatening those opposed to current logging practices.

Fortunately, not everyone reacts with violence, and many

Fortunately, not everyone reacts with violence, and many valley residents hope that a compromise of sustainable, sensible timber harvest will result in a stable timber industry, and neighbors who are able to sit down and talk over differences or amicably agree to disagree.

PHYLLIS LEFOHN

Above: *Beargrass, Skalkaho Pass.*
Right: *Brightly colored prayer symbols adorn the Medicine Tree.*

valley residents hope that a compromise of sustainable, sensible timber harvest will result in a stable timber industry, and neighbors who are able to sit down and talk over differences or amicably agree to disagree.

Highway 38 crosses Skalkaho Pass in the Sapphires and descends along the West Fork of Rock Creek. The short Centennial Grove Nature Trail displays signs interpreting the forest life along the trail. Thimbleberries were ripe and delicious, and tall dried stalks of an unmistakable and odd wildflower drew my attention—the pinedrop.

Pinedrops grow only in the shady forest, usually under pine trees. They cannot manufacture chlorophyll, and so lack the characteristic green color of most plants. They are a reddish-pink from top to bottom. The small dark scales on the bare-looking stalks are actually leaves; apple-like dried flower ovaries hang down from the top of the stalks. Fungi on the roots break down other plant matter, and the pinedrops feed off the decomposing materials.

There are a number of precipitous drop-offs as the road climbs the pass, and no guard rails for an illusion of safety. Take note: it could be a white-knuckle trip for the faint-hearted.

Skalkaho is a Salish word for beaver, and the Sapphires are full of suitable streams for that industrious critter. One of those streams drops abruptly to form lovely Skalkaho Falls. The road curls around next to the falls and travelers can get out and revel in the cold spray, or keep the windows rolled up and cruise slowly by.

The road over Skalkaho Pass provides an easy lesson in plant communities. The wetter, west side of the pass supports a lush understory of shrubs and flowers in the spruce and fir forest. The east side hosts dry-loving lodgepole pines which eventually taper off into fields of sagebrush and grasses.

Look for remnants of a water flume on the east side of the pass. These leftovers are reminders of unsuccessful attempts to mine vermiculite on Skalkaho Peak. Skalkaho Pass is along

WAYNE MUMFORD

Open country on the otherwise forested Skalkaho Road in the Pintler Range offers stunning scenery.

the western edge of the highly productive mining region of Montana.

The last dozen miles of this otherwise forested route roll through open country with stunning scenery. In the foreground, hay rolled into neat bundles looks like giant chunks of shredded wheat. To the south, across the rolling hills, the peaks in the Anaconda–Pintler Wilderness rise to alpine heights.

Those peaks are special places for many Montanans. I've climbed some, relentlessly putting one foot in front of the other to cross the steep talus slopes, glomming on to handholds and footholds while climbing up a vertical protrusion, crawling on hands and knees to peer over the edge of the summit and out beyond, onto hundreds of square miles of Montana. Worth every gasp for breath and each aching blister.

14 Rock Creek/Garnet Range

This backroads route wanders around atop the Sapphire block, a slab of the earth's upper crust that took several million years to slide from present-day Idaho to its current location. The Garnet Range, the Flint Creeks, the Anaconda–Pintlers, and the Sapphires outline that block. Magma forced its way into cracks in the block, and cooled into the mineral-rich veins that miners in this region have found very profitable.

The east-slope foothills of the Garnets produce a chert that prehistoric Indians valued for making arrowheads and tools. Hand-dug quarries here attest to thousands of years of mining the useful Avon chert. Later miners found garnets, gold, silver, and other metals in the mountains. The town of Garnet in the center of the range is one of Montana's best-preserved ghost towns.

Avon is the Welsh word for river. The Little Blackfoot River flows near this small community en route to merging with Warm Springs Creek. They form the Clark Fork and eventually these waters reach the Pacific Ocean. Stop at the Avon Family Cafe for a good bowl of chili and tasty pumpkin pie. It's a clean, wholesome sort of place, a pleasant roadside stop.

North of Avon, Highway 141 traverses the valley between the Garnet Range on the west and the Continental Divide to the east. Big haystacks adorn the rolling pastures; willows mark the course of Nevada Creek; livestock grazes the golden grasses; spruces and pines grow on the hillsides; the stunning, snow-clad peaks of the Scapegoat Wilderness rise to the north. It's a classic western Montana scene.

The bartender at the Copper Queen Saloon in Helmville was mixing somebody a mean-looking Bloody Mary. Graffiti covered the ceiling. A few patrons were throwing horseshoes outside in the pits next to the beer garden. The saloon is sandwiched between a maze of loading chutes and pens, and the old Copper Queen Hotel.

Architecture enthusiasts will enjoy the turn-of-the-century barns and houses in the area. Gable and gambrel rooflines, V-notched and square-notched logs provide clues to the German and Irish origins of early settlers. The only new-looking things in Helmville were the delightful stained-glass windows in the Catholic church. Worshippers may be reminded of the interconnectedness of all life as they gaze on clowns and other humans, penguins, flowers, zebras, stars, and water.

There wasn't much vehicle traffic on the Helmville–Drummond Road, but the pinball-course of cow plops attested to its bovine use. It looked like the whole ranch family, as well as various neighbors and relatives, were out for the occasion of moving cows. Three-foot-tall kids galloped around atop full-size horses, shooing the calves away from fences and back onto the road. Adults urged the bewildered calves forward, shouting over the bawling and grunting and adding to the general mayhem. Several pickup trucks idled along in front and behind, dispensing hot drinks. It looked like everyone was having a good time except the cows.

Drummond is located at the head of Flint Creek Valley, prime grazing country for over a century. Drummond's identity is tied up with cattle. Specifically, bulls. The cafe, stores, and even an apartment house use cow-related logos or names, and livestock yards right in town attest to the industry here.

The road south on Highway 1 is designated the Pintler Scenic Route. Open pasture butts up against forested hills; the absence of sagebrush is conspicuous; cultivated hay greens the valley bottoms; mountains rise on every side.

Stop in Philipsburg—"P-burg" to locals—for at least an afternoon. Residents have painted and spiffed up buildings, and the main street business district is very attractive. A self-guided tour points out 32 historic residences and businesses and tells a little story about each; Granite

County Museum and Historical Center displays an excellent collection of black and white photographs of ghost towns and Philipsburg history; empty storefronts have exhibits of minerals and historic artifacts that take the barren feeling away from vacant display windows. Businesses that have survived seem to have diversity as their key: a saddlery shop also sold Christmas gifts; the photo store had plant and flower supplies.

P-burg's most famous resident ran repeatedly for president of the United States. Merrill K. Riddick traveled the nation by bus, stumping for his Puritan Epic Party, pushing the concept of magnetohydrodynamics, and accepting no donations over a dollar per person. He died in 1988, still feisty at the age of 93.

At the top of Philipsburg's main street, Chris and Lillian Brown have renovated the Kaiser House and opened a restaurant. Built in 1887, the building served at different times as a court house, town hall, opera house, and library. Bars on the window in the men's room show the former jailroom; the women's room was once a documents vault. The restaurant is good, despite the lack of competition—it's the only one in the entire county. For lunch they offer sandwiches such as crab melts and French dips, or enchiladas; dinners are traditional steaks, salmon, prime rib, and seafood. The taco/burger/fruit/vegetable salad bar is a local favorite.

"We used to vacation in P-burg every summer before deciding to move here," Lillian said. "The people are so friendly. It's a nicer way of living. Here everybody knows everybody, and they're so helpful. I don't want to leave."

At the museum, pick up a brochure about Granite, then take a side trip up to the ghost town. The last mile is pretty iffy for passenger cars. You may wish to walk.

In the late 1800s, Granite was one of the world's richest silver areas, with 3,000 residents living in town. The history of the big silver strike is a Wild West story of Pony Express riders, blizzards, and tenacious hope.

There isn't much left of Granite today. Thistles blossom next to old stone foundations; wildflowers grow inside the old miner's hall. Sadly, several of the few remaining building were burned by vandals. The views of the surrounding mountains are quite pretty.

West of P-burg, Rock Creek's riffles and pools harbor five kinds of trout. The creek is one of Montana's most popular stream fisheries, and anglers are sometimes elbow-to-elbow during the big salmon-fly hatch each June. Even non-anglers stop to watch the spectacle of thousands of bright orange insects flitting above the creek or clinging to streamside shrubs.

The narrow road leads over forty miles of washboard bumps, through the forest and parks alongside Rock Creek. Cabins are scattered along its length. We drove by a great blue heron, standing stock-still less than thirty feet from a couple who were gathering cattails. Deer peered at us, then fled if we slowed down.

The light in this mountain valley is lovely. Aspen groves reflected a lime-yellow sunlight under their canopy; tall ponderosa pines dispensed a muted, tan light to the forest floor. Sparkles and glitters bounced off the water. Stop for a picnic, a walk, or a day of good fishing.

Even non-anglers stop to watch the spectacle of thousands of bright orange insects flitting above the creek or clinging to streamside shrubs.

GARRY WUNDERWALD

15 Snowy Mountains and Musselshell Country

I woke in the predawn—that magic time when you can feel the light arriving, but not yet see it. A lovestruck robin on the branch overhead wooed his intended with melodious trills. Deer stepped softly in the nearby meadow; the air was tranquil and cool; stars blazed in the dark sky.

Crystal Lake is an oasis in the prairie—not the mirage kind of oasis that disappoints you, but a real-life oasis of mountains, wildlife, greenery, moisture, wildflowers, and berries. Foot trails lead a few miles up to the crest of the Big Snowy Mountains. Hikers can walk the ridge, enjoy the extensive views, or climb into ice caves.

I was a month too early for strawberries. Judging by the abundant strawberry blossoms, you could come up and feast on the berries all day in late June or early July. Bluebells, violets, larkspur, spring beauties, lupines, and chickweed blossoms garnished the forested trail around the lake. Mallards cooed and murmured on their grassy nests until a doe and fawn coming to drink startled them into a honking escape. Two exquisite calypso orchids added a pink flourish to the wooded walk. A young buck's velvety nubs had sprouted out about three inches. I imagined them to be tender and sort of itchy-achy, like our gums feel when molar teeth come in.

Crystal Lake looked shallow enough to walk across. The surface along the shoreline bubbled and boiled as though fish were feeding on an insect hatch. I walked over to investigate and found springs bubbling up through the sandy bottom. Some were steady, pattering softly as they broke the surface. Others spurted irregularly and sounded like a child blowing bubbles in a glass of milk.

The road north out of Crystal Lake winds along the creek through aspens, willows, chokecherries, and wild roses. The bold lilac-pinks of hesperus and the bright sunflower-yellows of arrowleaf balsamroot peppered the hillsides. There are a few steep spots where the guardrails may fortify your courage.

Beavers have built dams up and down the stream. Fossils of oysters and other sea-dwelling creatures are hidden in the shale along roadcuts. Elk stopped browsing to watch me drive by, and red-winged blackbirds sang from the tops of cattails.

The road goes past the former Rock Creek School, now a private residence, then emerges from the canyon into the expanses of prairie. Silos punctuate the flat wheatfields; weathered farm buildings assume various angles of repose; the Judith Mountains and isolated buttes rise to the north.

Lewistown is an attractive community. A brochure available from the museum or the Chamber of Commerce provides a pleasant self-guided walking tour with short anecdotes and notes about historic buildings, including those in the silk stocking district. You can visit the Central Montana Museum and Lewistown Art Center, and drive out to ghost towns in the surrounding mountains. The city park has shade trees, tennis courts, and room to run and play. The missile mounted next to the playground was a bit unsettling.

Take 1st Avenue south to reach Route 238. Then a one-mile side trip on Route 466 leads to the lush greenery at Big Springs Fish Hatchery, located at one of the largest freshwater springs in the world.

Moisture that falls on the Big Snowies and the Judiths gets funneled underground, then gushes out here. The pure, cold water is ideal for raising over 2 million trout and salmon each year.

It was fascinating to look in the hatchery runs. The water literally seethed with fingerlings. They behaved like a single organism, racing frantically away from my silhouette like some thousand-tentacled octopus.

Two of us walked abreast, one on each side of the raceway, to see how they would respond. Predictably, they swam quickly down to the other end, but then those little brains couldn't figure out how to return since one of us was on each side. They bunched up at the end until the topmost fish were almost completely out of the water. One took the big chance and swam past, and suddenly the whole panicked pack was racing behind. Inter-

Above: *Church in Forestgrove.*

Facing page: *Crystal Lake, an oasis in the prairie.*

esting to find that young fish are herd creatures. I had thought of trout as solitary, defending their choice cutbanks and deep holes from intruders. Perhaps that comes with age and size.

The backroads route runs between the Big and Little Snowies, climbing gently to Flatwillow Divide for a fine view of Old Baldy rising to 8,678 feet, west of the road. Red Hill Road takes you into Lavina. The views south extend across the prairies and buttes in suitably-named Golden Valley County. The Absaroka Range one hundred miles south has an element of unreality from here. It's hard to distinguish if the peaks are snowy or if a bank of clouds has settled atop the range.

The prairie was lively with colors and sounds and movements. The unmistakable songs of meadowlarks carried across the fields on the breeze. Bold, white wing-stripes marked the numerous lark buntings flitting across the road. Hundreds of songbirds along the road watched me approach, then flew up and away at the last possible moment. I watched a prairie falcon in what can only be described as exuberant flight: it arced up to a point, twirled, then dove and arced up again to another twirl, again and again and again. A ferruginous hawk was more business-like, flying low and hunting intently, then soaring to scan for more possibilities. Prickly pears sent out yellow blossoms and vetch bloomed in clusters of bright purple. Two sharp-tailed grouse raced ahead of my vehicle for a long way before finally swerving off into the field.

A short side trip on Emory Road brings you to the 1915 Barlow Higgins homestead house, and the Emory School-house. The visitor register recorded celebrants' names from the 1991 Emory–Twin Coulee Reunion as well as the signatures of people from Wisconsin, Oklahoma, Washington, Pennsylvania, and even Alaska. I wonder if these folks trace family ties here, or if, like me, they were just lost on a back road and happened upon this delightful place.

Lavina's former glory days as an important stagecoach station for traffic moving between Billings and Lewistown is still discernible in the imposing size of the Adams Hotel. But today's travelers are more likely to stop twenty miles east in Roundup where businesses are clustered around the intersection of U.S. Highway 12 and U.S. Highway 87. Abandoned buildings near the railroad depot reveal the former business center, from a time when transportation was still rail- and horse-based, and mining coal and shipping cattle by rail were the biggest industries here.

The high, shrill whistles of killdeer rang across the water at Lake Mason National Wildlife Refuge, northwest of Round-up. One limped ahead of me, dragging a wing pathetically. As always, I immediately felt pity and wanted to follow it to help, then caught myself before I completely fell for the expert killdeer act of luring interlopers away from nests.

American avocets, Wilson's phalaropes, and other shorebirds strolled the banks. The smell of sodden vegetation and the noisy cries of gulls reminded me of the beach. Black-necked stilts strode around the shore, far to the north of their usual territory. Perhaps the strong spring winds blew them here, as it did the painted lady butterflies this year.

The route runs in long straight shots across the fields, with numerous abrupt corners and turns as it wends to Tyler, and back to Lewistown. Around Tyler, the road goes through the N Bar Ranch, an unusual cattle and grain business.

Tom Elliott took over the N Bar in 1964, and has systematically converted the operation to sustainable, organic methods of agriculture. Buyers still come from all over the West to buy the famous N Bar bulls at the twice-yearly sales, but he has expanded the ranching operations. Elliott runs the ranch according to his belief that diversity is the key to balance, both in nature and in human life. In addition to bulls, Elliott raises and markets beef cattle, Angus breeding stock, sheep, honey, eggs, organic produce, alfalfa, organic wheat, flax, oats, barley, canola, black medic, buckwheat, and timber. He also has an outfitting and guest program.

Keep your windows down. The smells change from field to forest, and birds sing and call from tree and fencepost. It's simply a delight.

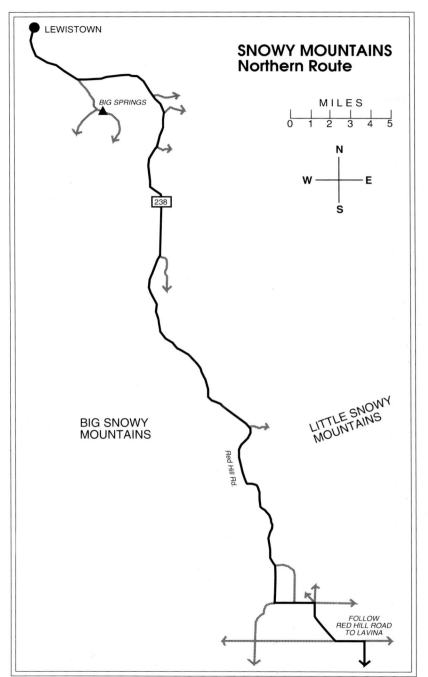

SNOWY MOUNTAINS
Northern Route

LEWISTOWN

BIG SPRINGS

238

MILES
0 1 2 3 4 5

N
W E
S

BIG SNOWY
MOUNTAINS

LITTLE SNOWY
MOUNTAINS

Red Hill Rd.

FOLLOW
RED HILL ROAD
TO LAVINA

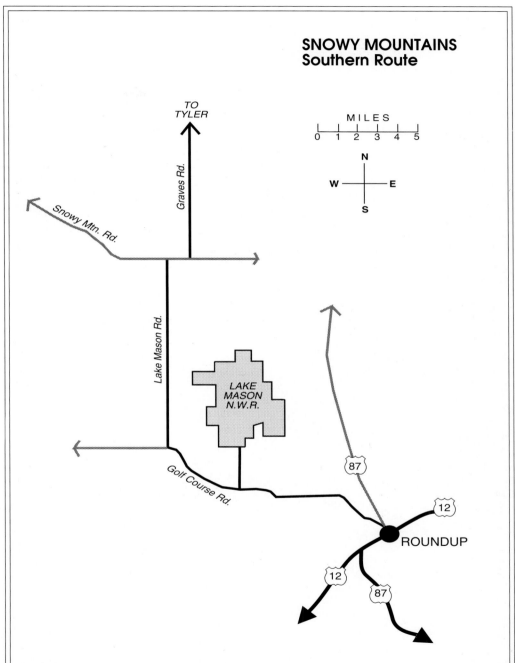

SNOWY MOUNTAINS
Southern Route

TO
TYLER

Graves Rd.

Snowy Mtn. Rd.

MILES
0 1 2 3 4 5

N
W E
S

Lake Mason Rd.

LAKE
MASON
N.W.R.

Golf Course Rd.

87

12

ROUNDUP

12

87

"The current methods of farming and ranching don't work in the long run," Elliott said. "Pesticides and herbicides and chemical fertilizers produce quick short-term results but ultimately stress the system. The infestation of leafy spurge here indicates a system out of balance. Rather than spraying poisons on it, which also kills or weakens the surrounding native vegetation, we're using sheep to graze it intensively, and cooperating with researchers to test some spurge-eating bugs.

"The first year the bugs were a total flop, as far as we could tell," he recalled. "The second year they ate and killed about a three-foot diameter area around the stake. This year they've killed about one hundred feet around it, and you can see fingers spreading out like a sunburst. They just reproduce themselves and eat spurge, then burrow into the roots for the winter, which also kills the spurge. It's very exciting."

Elliott estimates it will be at least twenty years before the spurge bugs and the intensive sheep-grazing will bring the rangeland back into balance. He's willing to wait.

The road north out of Tyler climbs up onto a high bench, with views of the Judith Mountains and extensive grasslands. I stopped to take photos, and a sheepherder across the field hopped on her horse and cantered over for a chat about the weather, sheep, and good books.

Grassrange was named for the nutritious native grasses covering the rolling hills and prairie lands in the productive Judith Basin. Once through Grassrange, the road winds through the bottomlands along McDonald Creek to Forestgrove, where the immaculately-kept little church joins my list of Montana's most picturesque buildings.

The road rises and falls with the contours of the land. Your perspective changes with it, ranging from big views into the distance, to closer, up-front looks at nearby fields, where cock pheasants strut and chuckle. Keep your windows down. The smells change from field to forest, and birds sing and call from tree and fencepost. It's simply a delight.

Above: *The pure, cold water of Big Springs is ideal for raising trout and salmon.*

Facing page: *Autumn reaches the Big Snowy Mountains.*

16 Marysville–Mullan Pass

Marysville is a funny mix that doesn't quite fit any category. It's mostly a ghost town, but about eighty people live here year-round. The humpy tailings from old placer mines line the creek, while ski lifts hum on the slopes above town. Burned-out foundation remnants of a huge stamp mill litter a hillside near diners enjoying steak and seafood dinners at the one and only business establishment.

Ann Korting and her dog Critter escorted me to Ruby Bastian's back porch, which doubles as the Marysville post office. Then we all strolled around town while they told stories of the old days in Marysville.

The town was named for Mary Ralston, the first woman who lived here. In its heyday, the 7,000 residents had 21 saloons to choose from. Ruby pointed to a decrepit, windowless building and told of eating ice cream at a marble counter there, sitting on fine wrought-iron chairs. "Next to it was the nicest dry goods store you ever saw," she said. "You could get everything at any time, even overshoes in July. In a big town you can't even get overshoes in March now."

Ann taught school in Marysville for twenty years. Now seventy-five years old, she teaches in nearby Helena. Ann played on the Marysville women's softball team in the 1940s, competing with rivals in Helena, York, Gould, and elsewhere. "Softball has a long tradition here. In the late 1800s Marysville had the best men's team in the Northwest," she stated. "They played teams as far away as Portland."

Today the only softball games at the town's ballfield are pickup games, usually when someone is having a big family gathering. With most of the residents past retirement age, softball takes a back seat to quiet hobbies and watching sunsets.

We walked through the old schoolhouse, where the relief maps on the walls caught my eye. When is the last time you've heard of Cape Colony, Galla Land, Persia, Athabasca, or Assinipoia?

Both Ann and Ruby belong to the Marysville Pioneers.

The Pioneers have preserved much of Marysville's history, maintained the old schoolhouse, erected historic markers around this semi–ghost town, and sponsored annual Marysville Days. Last year 78-year-old Ruby was honored for being the oldest Pioneer at the party.

The Pioneers are volunteers, and dues were one dollar a year when they formed in 1957. "Several members were quite peeved when we raised it to two dollars," Ann laughed.

More than $3 million worth of gold was placer-mined from nearby areas in the latter 1800s. But the biggest strike was the underground Drumlummon Mine, which produced $50 million worth of gold and silver between 1885 and 1910. Marysville boomed—then busted when the silver panic of 1893 hit. In February 1908 the entire business district burned, dealing the final blow to prosperity here.

Marysville is worth a visit. Walk around town or ski the slopes, then savor dinner and a brew at the Marysville House. Their outdoor barbecue goes Tuesdays through Saturdays, rain or snow. You can't beat the T-bones, served with ranch-style beans, corn on the cob, and mushrooms.

The road north out of Marysville climbs Trinity Hill and winds through the forest down to the arid valleys. The view across the upper meadows reaches to Lake Helena and the Big Belt Mountains. Grassy hills are dotted with typical dryland wildflowers: yarrow, mullein, coneflowers, yellow sweet clover, and thistles.

In winter this is a great cross-country skiing road. Local mushers like to work their huskies on it too. There are few sights lovelier than watching a team of dogs silently and joyfully pulling a sled across the white expanse.

Silver City sits at the center point of this figure-eight backroads route. A small lumber mill operates here, and you can find refreshments at the Silver City Bar and Cafe. Local cattle brands adorn the white acoustic ceiling tiles and wall paneling, a wood stove heats the place, and Edna's Hog Troff has classic greasy-spoon fare plus occasional specials. There's usually a local ready to share conversation if you belly up to the log-slab bar.

Trains are the best part of driving the Austin Road over Mullan Pass. You'll feel like you know the engineer and caboose man by the end of the trip, as you cross and recross the railroad tracks for 10 miles. Get out your camera, because it's one of the most picturesque railroading scenes you may ever see.

The railroad and the automobile road wind along the creek bottom and ascend the pass, following the original military road built in 1858-63 by, naturally, Lieutenant John Mullan. He first crossed this pass in 1854, driving a four-mule team and wagon. The entire Mullan Road was 624 miles long, connecting Fort Benton to Fort Walla Walla in Washington. Wagons hauling freight between the two forts averaged about 13 miles a day. If you take a leisurely drive through here, conserving your springs and shocks, you'll likely average a bit more than that in less than an hour of travel.

Except for the cattle and the clearcuts, the area probably looks much the same today as when Mullan came through. Broad open parks are ringed by forest, willows line the small creeks, deer and moose browse along the fringes. Wildflowers are abundant after the snow melts off. Pronounced like the lieutenant's surname, the mullein plant sends stalks skyward throughout the area. The dried stalks make great javelins when you're out for a picnic or a walk.

The mullein is an interesting plant. Despised by many because it looks "weedy" and freely colonizes disturbed roadside areas and overgrazed pastures, mullein has historic uses (as well as being a great toy). The name probably derives from the old English word "moleyne," meaning soft. Hummingbirds line their little nests with the soft hairs from the leaves. Ancient Romans and Greeks dipped the tall flower spikes in tallow and burned them as torches, and the Roman

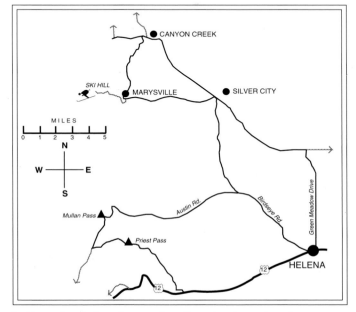

ladies colored their hair with yellow dye from the plant. American Indians knew its medicinal uses for easing rheumatism and respiratory ailments.

In another example of Montana's sometimes startling attentiveness to white history, a plaque in the middle of absolutely nowhere atop Mullan Pass commemorates the first Masonic meeting ever held in Montana.

Just a few miles away as the crow flies, Priest Pass lies nearly forgotten between the railroading Mullan Pass and U.S. Highway 12 over MacDonald Pass. Valentine Thomas Priest charged a dollar for a horse and wagon to cross his toll road. After a good rainstorm, you'll note that the washboarding is probably about the same today as it was one hundred years ago. Fortunately, today we don't have to pay a toll to drive this bumpy forested route back to Helena.

Trains are the best part of driving the Austin Road over Mullan Pass. You'll feel like you know the engineer and caboose man by the end of the trip, as you cross and recross the railroad tracks for 10 miles. Get out your camera, because it's one of the most picturesque railroading scenes you may ever see.

Right and facing page, left: Marysville.

Facing page, top right: Spring frost.
Bottom right: Tipi burner at Silver City.

17 Rocky Mountain Front

Travel parallel to the Continental Divide, moving across the foothills and prairie lands east of the mountainous divide. Grassy buttes rise from the plains; shallow lakes harbor waterfowl; deer and pronghorn antelope graze alongside horses and cows. And always, the mountains rise to the west.

The mountains are riveting. They shoot abruptly skyward, harboring grizzlies and elk, forests and alpine meadows. For some people, it is enough just to look and know they are there, wild and immense. Others shoulder backpacks, or saddle horses, and go in to learn the trails, fish the remote lakes, feel and live the wildness.

The Rocky Mountain Front hosts the largest uninterrupted piece of wilderness remaining in the contiguous United States. From the Scapegoat Wilderness on the south, wilderness designation protects the mountains north through the Bob Marshall and Great Bear wildernesses into Glacier National Park. It is a fantastic and unique resource.

Highway 434 climbs out of the stream bottom in Wolf Creek Canyon, and runs across the big open country adjacent to the Scapegoat Mountains. The views are stunning. The low-lying Adel, or Birdtail Mountains sprout spiny volcanic ridges that jut up through the grassy hills. Scattered ponderosa pines on the ridges are bent and contorted by the wind.

Horses grazed, tails to the wind, or galloped, heads and tails high, racing the wind and each other. Bluebirds sang from the fences, celebrating their egg-filled nests safe in the numerous birdhouses nailed to fenceposts along the road. Seven bull elk were silhouetted on a ridgeline, from spike-antlered adolescents to impressive, branch-antlered elders. Snow filled the draws, reflecting a low gleam onto the surrounding spring grasses.

The Bay Ranch has pastures on both sides of the road. The house and barns are tucked into a coulee, out of the wind. Mike Bay had spent the frosty morning calving. One young cow out by the creek wouldn't let her newborn suck, so we pushed/carried/coaxed the calf through the field to the corrals by the house. The anxious mother followed closely, bawling and protesting. Mike pushed the mother into a metal squeeze chute and tied her hind leg back, effectively trapping her into an immovable position. He then carried the confused calf to the cow, and, holding its mouth near the teats, started milking.

Milk squirted and dribbled all over the calf's face. After tentatively licking a few drops from its lips, that calf was a willing learner. Once the young mother got over her indignant resistance and let the calf nurse, Mike released her and she settled down to be a good mother, washing and nudging her youngster.

"This is one of the prices ranchers pay for breeding young cows," Bay said. "We all do it, but these first-time mothers sometimes need a lot of help. Others are real naturals and do everything easily."

Bay lives in Helena with his wife and son, and divides his time between outfitting and guiding fly fishing trips, and working the family's ranch. The two professions mesh well. Calving finishes about the time fishing begins, the cows and calves graze and grow all summer while he's on the rivers, then the fishing season ends and it's time to round up the cows. Some are sold and shipped, while others are kept to produce next year's calves. Winter means feeding and watering stock, and working on accounting and sales for the outfitting business.

Like most of Montana's unpaved back roads, this route between Highway 200 and Augusta is a sloppy, sometimes impassable mess when wet. If it *is* passable, you'll be captivated by the scenery and recreation opportunities. Haystack Butte pops out of the prairie near the mountain front. Most of the mountains are monolithic limestone slabs that slid to this location, but cone-shaped Haystack is igneous, a remnant of volcanic activity.

The Diamond Bar X is located at the confluence of Falls Creek and the Dearborn River, just west of Bean Lake. It has cabins, a decent restaurant, swimming pool, and horseback trips into the Scapegoat Wilderness. It's a nice, family-oriented operation.

The oldest rodeo in Montana takes place in Augusta. It's so popular and sometimes rowdy with celebrants that local business owners have been known to board up their big display windows, just in case. Mostly it's just a lot of people having a peaceable, great time at a rollicking good rodeo.

A side trip west toward Gibson Dam provides a quick lesson in the geology of this part of the Rocky Mountain Front. The first sight is a big glacial moraine. Moraine is the rocky debris pushed aside as a glacier flows out of the mountains and spreads across the plains. Then you'll drive through Sun River Canyon, a narrow, river-carved gorge in the limestone slabs of the mountains. The canyon widens and narrows several times, according to the age and resistance of the rock formations. Look at the roadcuts to see the sandwiched layers of sedimentary rock that were thrust up from horizontal to nearly vertical.

Choteau retains an Old West atmosphere downtown. Jeans, cowboy boots and cowboy hats are standard garb. Three backpackers with fishing rods walked across the main street, and a group of teens waited under the neon at the Roxy movie theater. The community goes all out for festivities. June—dinosaur celebrations. July—Rodeo, 4–H Fair, and Art on the Green. September—Antique Steam Engine Threshing Bee. December—Traditional Christmas Celebration. February—Winterfest.

The sundaes are excellent at the ice cream parlor in Choteau's Teton Trail Village. The "village" is a group of historic buildings, now housing shops and a small museum with dinosaur bones and area artifacts.

The areas west of Choteau are rich in wildlife, archeology, and geology. The Nature Conservancy's Pine Butte Swamp Preserve protects the last plains-dwelling grizzlies in the lower 48 states, as well as an incredible wetlands ecosystem. You can learn more at a roadside kiosk, or by staying at the very nice guest ranch located on the preserve.

Egg Mountain archeological site yielded the world's first discovery of baby duckbill dinosaurs. The 17 babies discovered here provided the first indication that dinosaurs cared for and nurtured their young. Public tours are led at 2 P.M. all summer. If you're *really* interested, sign up for a two-day or week-long course, and look for fossils with the experts.

Katy is the outspoken barkeep at Katy's Wildlife Sanctuary in Bynum. Bunnyrabbit and shamrock shoulder-tattoos showed through her blouse. She was entertaining the locals when we walked in. She grabbed my dusty sunglasses from the counter and splashed a bit of gin on each lens. "Gin cleans glasses better than any glass cleaner," she stated. "'Course, I can't do nothing about the chunks you got sandblasted in here."

We sat and listened to stories for a while, then continued down the highway. A Hutterite boy, complete with severe black hat and suit, walked on the shoulder towards home, head down into the wind. A few miles later, we watched a cock pheasant walk down the same road, head also down into the wind, also ignoring us. Mule deer grazed, knee-deep in a hay field.

I turned off Highway 89 at the border of the Blackfeet Indian Reservation, and headed west and north down the back roads, through Heart Butte to Browning. Families were enjoying summertime tailgate picnics at the little lakes outside Heart Butte. Kids raced around, and took turns riding double on a patient horse. It looked like everybody had a fishing line in the water.

Late in the day, the long rays of the sun lit the lake with gold, while dark clouds gathered off to the east. Looking east, we could have been on the Great Plains in any of the Northern Tier states. But to the west, the unmistakable outline of the Rocky Mountain Front was backlit by a spectacular red sunset.

Browning is the agency headquarters for the reservation. Plan to spend a few hours at the excellent Museum of the

Those of us who balk at *ding-donging* through the wilderness have learned to sing out when approaching thickets, or to talk rather louder than usual, or simply to live with the fact that we are not the highest link in the food chain here. It keeps you humble.

Right: *Perfect stillness at Castle Reef.*
Below: *Elk Creek, near Augusta.*

Plains Indians. The permanent displays and the changing exhibits are informative and interesting. The shop offers contemporary Native American arts and crafts. We watched a Navaho man carve beautiful flutes that had ornate bird and feather decorations. Lovely.

Glacier Park Lodge at East Glacier was built by the Great Northern Railway in the early 1900s as part of a network of accommodations for tourists. People arrived by rail and stayed at the lodge, then set out on long, backcountry horseback treks through the park. They stayed at hotels, chalets, and tent camps, eventually ended up at West Glacier, then rode the train back to East Glacier. A very civilized approach to the wilderness.

Today's backcountry traveler is more likely to carry a backpack, dried food, and a tent. Many wear bear bells.

The idea of a bell tied to foot or backpack is to alert bears that a hiker is coming. A startled bear is most likely to attack, so many hikers reason that while footsteps are very quiet, the bear will hear the bell from some distance, and hopefully vamoose into the forest.

Those of us who balk at *ding-donging* through the wilderness have learned to sing out when approaching thickets, or to talk rather louder than usual, or simply to live with the fact that we are not the highest link in the food chain here. It keeps you humble.

Dallas Koehm is a backcountry ranger in Glacier. "People are certainly innovative about making noise to alert bears," he chuckled. "One fellow carried a boom box on top of his pack, and played it full blast along the trail. Somebody else had a big ol' cowbell. Others blow whistles intermittently. But the all-time winner was a guy with a drum. I heard that big booming from a mile away, and thought maybe some super grouse had developed a new technique to attract the females.

"That drum was certainly effective," he concluded. "I didn't see a single creature for miles around."

Sheri Courtney owns the Thimbleberry Restaurant in East Glacier. She has 29 employees during the summer season. Twenty-two of them are enrolled members of the Blackfeet tribe.

"I originally ate here as a tourist," Courtney said. "I loved the building and the hummingbirds and the lawn. This is a fabulous way to live. There's no place like the park in summer, and in winter I can go anywhere and lead a city life if I want."

The restaurant is built of logs, and has big picture windows overlooking a little aspen grove. Tall pines stick up through the roof gables outside, and inside it smells wonderful.

Each day the Thimbleberry staff makes and serves over ten gallons of chili; bakes up to 25 pies in five different flavors; picks thimbleberries for specialty muffins and cheesecakes; and cooks up lots of delicious Indian fry-bread. Soups are all made from scratch. You can't go wrong eating here.

Highway 49 between East Glacier and Kiowa is an orphan highway. The state doesn't want it, nor does the park. But it's there, it's still a ward of the state, and it's a beautiful drive along the western edge of the Blackfeet Indian Reservation.

En route to the Two Medicine area, I saw glacier lilies blooming in profusion under the forest canopy. Red-winged blackbirds flitted around a boggy area. The weight of a late spring snowfall had bent young aspens nearly to the ground.

The road parallels and crosses the Two Medicine River, traverses the side of a steep mountain, and provides views of the utterly spectacular peaks in Glacier. Rising Wolf Mountain makes a picture-perfect backdrop to the Two Medicine lakes. Two Medicine is one of the few areas where motorists can clearly see the spectacular red argillite rock layers on the peaks.

There are visitor facilities in several lakeside locations just off the backroad route. Take a side trip to Two Medicine, St. Mary, and Many Glacier. You can ride a guided-tour boat, hike numerous easy or difficult trails, relax and eat, and see the exhibits at the visitor center. The hotel at Many Glacier looks like a fantasy chalet creation from a Disney fairy tale. The famous Going-to-the-Sun Road traverses the scenic center of the park, climbs the Continental Divide from St. Mary, and drops down at West Glacier.

As you drive north through St. Mary to Babb, the road rises and falls, descending into a region of lakes, shrubs, and grasslands, then climbs back up into the forest where stunted aspens sprout out of the rocky soil. Beavers have dammed the streams into a series of pools and drops. The visual relief of the landscape is enchanting; the lakes and mountains defy description.

You'll make an abrupt transition to the Great Plains grasslands, where few fences and vast distances make it easy to envision riding a horse here for hours, the only obstacles being willow bottoms and forested slopes.

I stopped for a picnic along the road. Bluebells, violets, dandelions, white phlox, and buttercups bloomed in the field. Cows bellowed for their calves in a pasture below the road. Two huge silvertip grizzlies ambled across a field, rooting and digging for insects and roots. They were about half a mile away, but as the honey and cashew butter dribbled out of my sandwich onto my hands, I had a sudden daydream of an enormous, shaggy head appearing in front of me, sniffing with interest. It didn't take long to finish that sandwich.

Above: *Removing dinosaur bones at a dig near Choteau.*

Little Belt Mountains and Golden Triangle

The drive from Helena to York delivers a quick lesson in contemporary Western life. The pristine Gates of the Mountains Wilderness graces the northern skyline. But in the valley below, strip-type development littering Montana Avenue typifies the worst of the sprawling urban West. The street is narrow and traffic moves fast. Lack of sidewalks makes it intimidating to walk even a few hundred yards from one business to another. The mega-chains are moving in, paving acres of parking lots and installing enough outdoor lighting to make one wonder if the corporate owners think energy conservation is a quaint, irrelevant concept.

York Road travels through the Helena Valley, which has been carved into numerous 20-acre ranchettes to accommodate a bedroom community for Helena. Trailers and prefab houses mix with big old farmhouses and new architecture. Horses stand, bored, in small overgrazed fields, and the valley residents' seemingly obligatory dogs run alongside the vehicles, barking. Automatic yard lights dispense their beams from fifty-foot power poles, blocking the stars and the night from each house.

The farms remaining in the valley depend primarily on alfalfa hay and cattle. There are a smattering of other ventures, such as organic vegetables, hydroponic tomatoes, honeybees, and pigs. The innovative Lazy Daisy Dairy produces Grade-A raw milk, then delivers it right to your refrigerator, along with cheeses, organic produce, and foood staples.

Look for the Farm in the Dell along your route. This impressive residential farm for adults with developmental disabilities was built by volunteer community labor. In 1990 local residents and contractors got together for an old-fashioned house-raising, and completely built the shell in one weekend.

Each spring residents hand-plant and raise over 300,000 flower starts in the greenhouse and fields. They supply flowers for the tables of local restaurants year-round, and supply food to some state-run group homes in the area.

The Farm in the Dell employs 21 adults, and also teaches living skills such as cooking, laundry, and house cleaning. Combining their work experience and life skills, developmentally disabled residents who have spent their entire lives dependent on state-run group homes eventually may move into communities on their own, and find employment in greenhouses or on ranches.

Let it warm your heart a little as you drive by.

You'll likely see anglers trolling Hauser Lake, or fishing from shore near the York Bridge. The lake holds eight- to ten-pound walleyes, as well as rainbow and brown trout, and smallmouth bass. After crossing the York Bridge the road heads into a pretty little canyon. Scattered ponderosa pines and junipers cling to the dry hillsides, and limestone outcrops jut out on both sides. The willows lining Trout Creek color the streambanks in varying hues of gold, red and green.

The York Bar serves a juicy burger, and has a few groceries, a gas pump, and horseshoe pits. York bears absolutely no resemblance to its namesake, New York City. Nevertheless, residents of both New York, New York, and York, Montana can get a big laugh out of the annual riding-lawnmower race.

There are numerous small sapphire mines in the Hauser/ Canyon Ferry area. Enthusiasts can pan for these semiprecious gems at various public and private spots. Montana sapphires and agates are the state's official gemstones.

Between about Halloween and Christmas, the nation's official bird arrives. Bald eagles congregate by the hundreds to feed on spawning kokanee salmon. Riverside Recreation Area right below Canyon Ferry Dam is one of the best places to watch a bald eagle plunge into the icy water and laboriously flap off, talons clutching a wildly gyrating fish. Volunteers usually staff the area on weekends, and provide information and spotting scopes.

In summer, you'll share this same area with numerous anglers of the human and the feathered variety. Ospreys, golden eagles, and peregrine falcons cruise the air currents while pelicans and humans cruise the spillway currents. All display a remarkably similar demeanor, from bright carnivorous gleams in the eyes to laid-back, eyes-closed enjoyment of a sunny afternoon when the fish are presumably doing the same—out of reach.

One summer morning I watched five young golden eagles at Hauser Lake. They soared through the canyon with masterful grace, swooping and hovering and obviously delighting in playing with each other. Landing in trees was not so graceful though—that appeared to be an acquired skill. The eaglets sometimes made three or four awkward passes before completing a landing in some tall snag overlooking the river.

It had never occurred to me that they had to practice such things, so I watched with great amusement as they fished. They perched on large rocks in the river near shore, and watched the water with great intensity. Each would make an abrupt, splashing jump into the water, and emerge fishless. Their fishing expedition evoked a good deal of preening and shaking of feathers, but no sustenance. After a few hours of watching, I nearly felt sorry enough to throw them some of my catch. Nearly, but not quite.

The county road along the east side of Canyon Ferry Reservoir provides beautiful vistas west over the blue waters to the Elkhorn Mountains. To the east, numerous seasonal streams carve miniature canyons into the Big Belt Mountains. One of the gulches shelters prehistoric pictographs on the rock walls. Another shows the scarred remains of a forest fire. Yet another holds my memories of working for the Forest Service one spring, planting fir and pine seedlings in the slushy, half-frozen earth. On this 95-degree day, it was hard to summon up the memory of fingers so cold they wouldn't uncurl enough to grasp a six-inch seedling, of laughing with co-workers as we slowly thawed out at lunch breaks, of pushing the van through snowdrifts to get to the planting areas.

Confederate Gulch Road intersects the county road at milepost 26. It's a narrow, winding, bumpy route through the Big Belts. Forget hurrying. Don't tow a trailer or drive your big RV. Do take a picnic, a Helena National Forest map, a camera, and a good spare tire.

Confederate Creek has numerous beaver dams and lots of places to watch the beavers maintaining them. The cottonwoods and willows make the stream-bottom lush compared to the adjacent dry slopes of sage, juniper, and scraggly ponderosa pine. Look for wild raspberries, strawberries, and gooseberries to sweeten your picnic.

Numerous captured Confederate soldiers banished up the Missouri swarmed over Montana Territory in the 1860s. Piles of rocks attest to the frenetic mining activity that once nearly consumed this gulch. The Montana Bar claim yielded $1,000 to $2,000 worth of gold per panful. Twenty miners panned 700 pounds of gold from that two-acre claim in one day.

Diamond City, now obliterated by hydraulic mining debris, once held 10,000 residents intent on wealth. They had to build their houses on stilts to avoid being buried by tailings washed down from above. The area produced about $17 million in gold in about six years, then nearly everyone left. A few weekend gold miners work the area these days. Optimism springs eternal.

After crossing the forested Big Belts, the route turns north and meanders across the hilly golden grasslands, the road winding like a ringlet twining down a woman's back.

Janis Joplin's "Summertime" played as the sun shone through the open car window and burned my left forearm and shoulder. Memories of past river trips popped into mind while I gazed east across the pastures and over the Smith River Canyon to the Little Belts. I've had the best and the worst times while floating the Smith, from "blissed-out" diving into the deep, still pools, to huddling against a driving sleet and help-

Riverside Recreation Area right below Canyon Ferry Dam is one of the best places to watch a bald eagle plunge into the icy water and laboriously flap off, talons clutching a wildly gyrating fish.

85

lessly watching a whirlwind pick up the rafts and tents and toss them upriver.

This is truly beautiful country. The big ranches have open, unfenced range that provides teasing glimpses of how the land must have looked before white settlement. Deposits of red soil alternate with tan—like driving on a gigantic peppermint stick. Pronghorn antelope gallop away at the sight of a vehicle; bluebird boxes cling to the fenceposts; hills undulate across the miles to the mountains.

The dust on my sunglasses was deep enough to write messages in. I rinsed them in the Smith River under Eden Bridge, and picked the prickly seeds and needle-and-thread grass out of my shoelaces so they would untie. Sitting in the warm water, I lunched on tuna while trout fingerlings nibbled my toes.

Not many people go to Stockett, Sand Coulee, Centerville, or Tracy. They're not on the way to much of anywhere, so not many have reason to drive through.

These tiny, next-door-neighbor communities are about 10 miles from Great Falls. The area's coal-mining heritage is reflected in Centerville's centerpiece: the giant fan used to ventilate the Griffen Mine in 1884. A tiny coal car sits outside the high school, whose sports teams are called the Miners.

Coal mined here fueled the Great Northern Railroad until electric, natural gas, and diesel replaced coal in the latter 1920s. Today, most residents are retired or work in Great Falls. The Yatsko family in Stockett pops and delivers nearly all of Great Falls' ready-to-eat popcorn. You can sample Yatsko's Popcorn in the Centerville Bar, where you'll be served a heaping portion in a red dog bowl.

The American Bar is Stockett's real community hall. The fluorescent lights blaze as bright as a gymnasium from opening until closing time at 10 P.M. Local families come in for libation, gossip, sandwiches, shuffleboard and bowling games, or to get a loaf of bread or carton of milk.

Don't stop here if you're in a hurry. Do stop if you're hungry or thirsty. Owner Brian Guisti carefully slices the meat and builds you a very fine sandwich. Be sure to order horseradish on the side. He'll also serve your beer in a frosty mug, and stack a huge ice-cream cone for the road. If it gets too busy, the regulars will jump up and help out until things settle down.

Claire Roehm was alongside the road, picking ripe stalks of wheat for a bouquet. We stopped to talk a bit about life in the Golden Triangle. Like most folks here, the Roehms grow barley and hard red winter wheat. Their combine moved deliberately down the rows of wheat, filling each truck with 50,000 pounds of golden ripe kernels. They harvest about one hundred acres a day, weather permitting. "When it's over we go home and collapse," Claire said.

The combine cab was remarkably quiet and cool, a good refuge from the incredibly noisy harvest. The harvester vibrated, equipment lights flashed, gauges and meters registered numbers, and a deluge of dust and debris filled the air as the kernels were gathered, cleaned, and funneled into the waiting grain trucks.

It was easy to see why farming is such a high-risk occupation. The hours are long and the equipment is massive, with innumerable parts that spin, chop, grind, suck, thrash, poke, and compress.

Farmers were harvesting in every direction as I drove north to ride the Carter Ferry across the Missouri River. Dust filled the air behind each working crew; pheasants ran across the road to hide in adjacent fields; neat orderly rows of silos were being filled to the tops; the Highwood Mountains backdropped the pastoral scene. This is the perfect realm for playing "The Long and Winding Road" as you drive.

Some of these county roads look suspiciously like two-track country lanes when the grass in the center strip brushes the undercarriage of your car. But somebody out there has

JOHN McNEAL

been busy with a paintbrush and just when you think you're definitely on the wrong road, an arrow buried in a stack of signs will provide assurance that it's the way to the ferry.

There's always a moment of apprehension when I descend into the river breaks and see the road end at the river's edge. But press the magic little button on the post, and within minutes the operator comes down to the river, and slowly brings the ferry across.

Bridges have inexorably replaced this delightful, seasonal, transport, and Carter has one of the last ferries operating on the Mighty Mo. Ron Haalend has operated this ferry for the

Above: *View from Square Butte, near Geraldine.*

Facing page: *Wheatfield near Canyon Ferry Reservoir.*

past four years. He makes 15,000 to 20,000 crossings a season before the ice closes the channel. His old dog Gringo hobbles down to meet each and every passenger. "Yeah, it's a good life," Haalend drawled. "They give me a good place to live here, and the people are all real friendly. I hope they don't go building a bridge here."

In Fort Benton, two retired pharmacists donated items from their collections and stocked and restored an old drugstore displayed at the Museum of the Northern Great Plains. A bare-breasted Indian maiden smiled from the box of Indian Compound of Honey Boneset and Squills, an elixir certain to ease "coughs, colds, and all affections of the throat and lungs." Her container was sandwiched between dozens of other remedies, such as Halibut Liver Oil; Cramp Bark Compound; and Obesoids, "30 day treatment for reducing fat."

The museum has big plans to fully furnish its pioneer village complex, and locals have responded enthusiastically. Numerous buildings have been brought in and restored by volunteer labor.

I peered in the filthy windows of an old house they've hauled in but not yet worked on. Water-stained wallpaper hung in shreds, the floors had broken boards, glass shards were everywhere. It didn't look like any fun at all to work on that one. Yet the buildings already opened for viewing are wonderful.

"It's mostly done by word of mouth," Shirley Scheele said. "People dig around and ask around until they find stuff. They've found all but two original pews for the little church, and even found the first altar rail."

Scheele has restored dozens of the antique farm implements displayed in the cavernous museum. MacBuff the tomcat stretched out on a wooden combine used between 1925 and 1940. That combine needed 32 horses to pull it. An excellent display explained all the steps used in hand-harvesting wheat, then showed the various pieces of equipment that re-

placed that hand work. Farm families used a scythe, cradle, and sickle, and then tied bundles and operated a fanning mill, flail and tread, and winnowing tray. When the work was finished, the family had only enough electrical power from the two-bladed windmill to either burn one light, or listen to the radio.

Scheele was working on an old disk-harrow, straightening bends, cleaning wire, and getting ready to prime and paint the implement with the original factory colors. "With these machines you learn how to do things by necessity. I think the hardest one was that big wooden combine," she said. "I had to build a new reel for the header part."

A few blocks away, the Museum of the Upper Missouri displays steamboat-era items. This museum will be incorporated into the new Bureau of Land Management Visitor Center to be completed in 1994. My favorite display had stagecoach travelers' tips from the 1877 Helena *Herald*: "Don't imagine for a moment that you are going on a picnic; Spit on the leeward side; If you have anything to drink in a bottle pass it around; Don't growl at the food received at the station; Don't point out where murders have been committed, especially if there are women passengers."

Fort Benton is a real treat for visitors. A half million bricks built the Grand Union Hotel into what was once the fanciest place in Montana on "the bloodiest block in the West." Fatal gunfights were commonplace along the levee in the 1860s, during the heyday of gold fever, steamboating, and minimal law enforcement Today the hotel stands vacant, awaiting someone with the money and vision to make it operable again. The Upper Missouri National Wild & Scenic River and Lewis and Clark Trail Visitor Center displays projectile points and dinosaur teeth as well as contemporary books and pictures. The Banque Club serves a decent meal; museum volunteers are full of anecdotes to enliven the displays; and the river itself holds the magic of all moving water.

A soft breeze chased the bugs away as I sat on the foot bridge and then strolled around reading the interpretive signs along the riverfront and in the park. These are not run-of-the-mill interpretive signs. They are really interesting, providing facts as well as humor.

Two RVs and three tents were set up in the park. Campers sat on their lounge chairs sipping coffee, shaded by the giant cottonwood trees. Children shouted and laughed in the city pool. Occasional odors of dead fish reminded us that the river was and is the central part of this pleasant community.

Any hint of the Missouri's existence disappears when you drive across the bridge and climb up onto the northern Great Plains. Square Butte and Round Butte pop out of the prairie east of the Highwood Mountains. The mountains and buttes are the hard remains of a volcano that erupted shonkinite and other materials 50 million years ago. A mere 70,000 to 130,000 years ago, a glacier pushed pieces of northern Manitoba onto the prairie, and ice dammed the Missouri River to make Glacial Lake Great Falls. That lake spilled over and carved a channel known as the Shonkin Sag, which runs along the north side of the Highwoods.

You can't mistake Geraldine for any other community. Big, colorful wooden letters welcome you to town, and cartoon characters and bows adorn the fences, the old depot, homes, and various walls around town. City maintenance worker Donnie Thomas made look-alikes from Disney films, Sesame Street, and Peanuts and Garfield comics. He was clearly a beloved member of this town—residents dedicated their city park to his memory.

This is still the Golden Triangle, where wheatfields stretch forever. A few farmers grow safflowers, whose thistly yellow blossoms smell a lot like cherry coke in the cool of an August evening. Greens and yellows dominate the view—lime greens of emerging wheat, deep greens of conifers, yellowish-greens of hay, grayish-greens of sage. Robins and meadowlarks sing on

Grand Union Hotel, Fort Benton.

WAYNE SCHERR

the fenceposts; water wizard mirages appear and disappear on the hot road surface; a few isolated buildings and barns dot the pastures and hayfields.

The buttes and mountains are visually intriguing. The forested tops rise above white, cliff-like outcrops and distinctive, parallel ridges of rocks that run down the sides like giant dinosaur spines. Lewis and Clark called similar formations on the Missouri "parallelepipeds." That term never caught on in the world of geology, but it remains one of my all-time favorite words.

It's clear that Round and Square Buttes were named by someone looking from the south. They bear no resemblance to either roundness or squareness from any other side. Shrubs and trees grow in the north-facing coulees, and grasses secure the dryer, hotter slopes. A high point on the road supplies an extended view over the prairie and scattered island ranges: Sweetgrass Hills, Little Rockies, Bears Paws, Little Belts, and Highwoods. This is beautiful country.

You'll travel on Kings Hill National Forest Scenic Byway, which cuts through the center of the Little Belt Mountains, runs alongside creeks, goes through old mining towns, and climbs a 7,393-foot pass.

The Cub's Den in Monarch does a brisk business with the prairie-dwelling folks who like to get into the mountains. The beer taps are buried in large tree trunks along the bar. Big windows provide a good view of the cliffs outside.

Don Croff had stopped in for a visit on his way to line camp. He ranches west of the Highwoods, and relishes time in the mountains. He also enjoys telling stories about summering his cattle around his line camp in the Little Belts. He described looking out the dusty window of his cabin one year and seeing the imprint of a mountain lion paw that was bigger than a man's hand.

"This summer we took a bunch of cow/calf pairs up, and turned 'em loose," he said. "One cow followed us to the cabin, and stood and stared—a long, level, distressed stare. She

followed me to the outhouse, and back to the cabin, always staring. For hours. So I finally got back in the truck, drove the 50 miles back to the pasture, and there was her calf bellowing away. I brought him back, and she walked away with him, very dignified. She knew who to blame for leaving her baby behind, all right."

This route has plenty of outdoor recreation opportunities, such as camping, fishing, picnicking, hiking, snowmobiling, and cross-country and downhill skiing. The reasonably-priced cafeteria at Showdown has the best-tasting lunches of any ski area in Montana.

Porphyry Lookout at the top of the ski hill provides good views of the whole region. Miners pulled more than $3 million worth of sapphires from area mines, as well as silver and lead.

Don't miss an outdoor soak in the natural hot pool at the Spa Motel in White Sulphur Springs. Places like this are the delights of Montana backroads—totally unpretentious and good value. For a few bucks you can float in warm blissful peace, any season, any weather. Do it.

Highway 12 cuts through Deep Creek Canyon, first climbing up through big open pastureland to a small pass in the Big Belts, then dropping down the narrow canyon alongside the creek. Roadcuts reveal white limestone and gray mudstone, and you can see where the rocks folded and buckled as they were pushed up from a valley floor into their current mountain shape.

Deep Creek Bar & Restaurant in this tiny bend in the narrow canyon serves a pleasant ending to a day. The well-kept, big, log structure sits right on the banks of the creek, and good, beefy Montana meals and occasional gourmet surprises are served. If you're feeling more cosmopolitan, Rosario's in Townsend provides excellent Italian cuisine and pizzas. It's easy to overlook small, inconspicuous Rosario's, but you'll find it if you're hungry—in Townsend on Highway 12, on the east side of the road.

You can't mistake Geraldine for any other community. Big, colorful wooden letters welcome you to town, and cartoon characters and bows adorn the fences, the old depot, homes, and various walls around town.

19 Flathead Indian Reservation

The Bread Board in Bigfork stacks its display case with freshly-made bread, muffins, rolls, and other baked delectables every morning. They also serve very good coffee with wholesome breakfasts and lunches. It's a delight to smell the bread baking as you munch an omelet or croissant.

I don't normally have a sweet tooth in the morning, but my table was right next to the display case. One piece of raspberry shortcake would be a perfect finish to breakfast. It was so good I then had a piece of huckle-cherry pie, and contentedly went out to waddle through galleries and art and crafts shops in town.

Bigfork is a water-oriented resort/hamlet with lots of tourist activities. Many of the resident artists display their paintings, pottery, and sculptures in local galleries. The popular playhouse theater produces Broadway musicals all summer. You can cruise or sail on Flathead Lake, participate in various Western-style ranch activities, and eat and shop to your heart's content.

Highway 35 runs down the east side of Flathead Lake, past cherry orchards, farms, forest, state parks, and lovely views of the lake.

Flathead Lake Biological Station is located on Yellow Bay, in a stand of virgin pine, larch, and Douglas fir. Aquatic biologists here study and monitor the wet parts of this region—lakes, ponds, swamps, bogs, spring brooks, streams, and rivers. Plant biologists have numerous habitats to study nearby—palouse prairie grasslands, montane fir, cedar and pine forests, subalpine meadows, and even tundra. Research from the station, which was established in 1896, has had a major impact on conserving and improving water quality in Flathead Lake.

Bowman Orchards has been on the lake a long time. Jerry Bowman grew up here, bought his dad's business, and expanded the operations. At 65 acres, his is the largest orchard in the Flathead. The average orchard size here is about four acres, but there are lots of one or two acre orchards too.

Bowman grows cherries. Lots and lots of cherries—sweet Lamberts, Lapins, and Rainiers, and tart Mont Morencies for pies. At harvest time, he and his wife and their three grown daughters work full-time, and employ up to 60 people to hand-pick every cherry.

"It's a challenge to grow cherries here," Bowman said. "We clear the land ourselves, plant and water, grow the cherries, pack them, and sell them directly to individual customers. My wife and daughters check the quality of every cherry we sell. It's nice being with the fruit when it gets to customers."

Bowman described the killing weather in January 1989 that almost wiped out the entire Flathead cherry industry. "I was out pruning in my shirt sleeves," he said. "You could see the cold air coming down the lake from Canada. Steam rose off the lake as that arctic air hit the water. I was almost frozen by the time I got back to the house.

"Then that terrible east wind started," he continued. "The cold and wind combined to damage the connective tissue in the trunks and limbs. Survival was a lot like with people—the old and young trees couldn't take it, but many of the rest made it. The ground didn't freeze so the roots survived, but every bud was dead."

Bowman said after that winter it would have been easy to say, "The heck with it," and get out of the business, but he was encouraged by the support and assistance he received for replanting. "It was heart-warming to know people care about this industry," he said. "I could really see that it's something special to Montanans."

Polson sits at the southern end of the lake. The Port Polson Players perform comedies and musicals each July and August, and the *Port Polson Princess* tour boat cruises the lake all summer. There are two museums—the Polson–Flathead Historical Museum, and the Miracle of America Museum. Polson-Flathead concentrates on area history, while the Miracle is a private tribute to patriotism, pioneers, and the

Besides bison, you are likely to spot elk, deer, bighorn sheep, and pronghorn antelope in the peace of the National Bison Range.

military. It is filled to the brim with everything from a sheep-powered treadmill invention, to armored vehicles, to buffalo rifles, to a 65-foot logging boat used on Flathead Lake.

South on Highway 93 leads across the Flathead Indian Reservation. The Mission Range fills the eastern horizon, above the grassy valley. Pablo and Ninepipe are glacial pot-hole wildlife refuges. Enthusiasts can take binoculars and field guides to birds and wildlife and have a ball at these undeveloped areas.

The Mission Mountain Wilderness is unique in America. It was the first area to be designated wilderness by an Indian nation on its own tribal lands. A roadside marker quotes Clarence Woodcock, speaking about the Confederated Salish and Kootenai Tribes' conviction that the mountains must remain protected in perpetuity: "They are lands where our people walked and lived. Lands and landmarks carved into the minds of our ancestors through coyote stories and actual experiences. Lands, landmarks, trees, mountain tops, crevices that we should look up to with respect."

It takes a minimum of several hours, and preferably the better part of a day, to visit the National Bison Range at Moiese. It's a bit disconcerting to see buffalo burgers for sale at the entrance to the range, but once past that, the visitor center and self-guided auto tour are very interesting.

The National Bison Range was established in 1908, barely in time to help save the entire species from total extinction. In a frenzy of rampant killing, Americans mercilessly slaughtered 50 million wild bison in just four decades. In 1900 only twenty wild bison were known to exist. The herd at the refuge was started with 41 bison that had been in captivity, to try to protect and preserve the last of this species.

Today there are about 350 bison on the preserve, as well as elk, deer, bighorn sheep, and pronghorn antelope. If the herds outgrow the capacity of the range to feed them, some animals are sold. The range also supports a variety of beautiful

wildflowers, especially abundant in springtime. Look for Montana's state flower, the bitterroot, on dry hills.

The Flathead River cuts a wide meandering swathe between Dixon and Perma. Spring snowmelt from the Missions gives it an extraordinary opaque blue color, a beautiful contrast to the open hills and islands.

Turn north on Highway 382 just past Perma, toward Camas. Tall mullein stalks line the road up the narrow drainage. You can see remnants of an old roadbed here before the highway leaves the draw and crosses Markle Pass. Stop at the pass and look carefully at the broad, open valley ringed by low mountains.

This area was once under Glacial Lake Missoula. Glacial Lake Missoula existed about 15,000 years ago when glacial ice blocked the Clark Fork. Water backed up to a depth of 2,000 feet and the volume of water was comparable to today's Lake Ontario. The ice dam eventually floated and broke up. Instead of a normal spillway over the top, a wall of water 2,000 feet high gushed out and the entire lake emptied in a matter of days—the greatest flood ever recorded by geologists. Boulders carried in that flood are wedged 1,000 feet above the river in the Columbia River Gorge and are still scattered across the Willamette Valley floor in western Oregon.

After the lake emptied, more glacial ice would again impound the river. The lake refilled and burst many times. From Markle Pass you can see the giant ripple marks made when the floods poured through the valley. They look just like the ripples on a stream bottom today, magnified manyfold. Some are 35 feet high.

Take a short side trip west to Hot Springs, "Home of the Famous Limp In Leap Out Hot Mineral Baths." Two "blissed-out" people sat in the little chutes at the "corn hole" and soaked their feet in the mud baths. A paunchy man opened his eyes long enough to tell me that the fine, silty mud soaked off corns and bunions, and made your feet really soft.

We hopped into a little hot pool near the abandoned

TOM DIETRICH PHOTOS

bath house. Two elderly women joined us for a while, then a bunch of kids and their mothers came in. One woman attested to the healing powers of the mud, telling of her horse's leg cut nearly to the bone at the hock. She packed it with the mud, and the horse healed fast, with no scar and no limp.

Someone's big plans for developing the hot pools had gone awry. A painted panorama of forest and stream was peeling off the abandoned bathhouse, windows were broken out and the doors boarded shut. But the grounds here are immaculate. Community volunteers keep it clean, and they obviously love the place. It's very simple, very neat, and very pleasant.

North of Hot Springs, you'll pass thick layers of light-gray silty hills eroding into a badlands look. These sediments are bottom deposits from Glacial Lake Missoula. North of the highway, Hog Heaven Hills are remnants of an ancient volcano. There are large deposits of silver in those hills.

The road crosses a big pile of glacial moraine and drops down for marvelous views of Flathead Lake and the Swan Range. Before completing the loop back to Polson, take a short side trip to Rollins to stock up on some of the best sausages in Montana.

M & S Meats and Sausages has its own herd of bison and cattle. M & S makes everything from turkey teriyaki jerky to buffalo thuringer, and smokes turkeys, hams, bacon, chicken and salmon. They even have Pennsylvania-style scrapple. The taste quality is no secret—M & S ships products all over the country, over 1,500 pounds of preservative-free jerky each week. Stop in for a meat treat. Chances are good you'll become another devoted customer.

Left: Fishing on Bigfork Bay, Flathead Lake.
Above: Cherry blossoms mean springtime in the Flathead.

20 Purcell Mountains Loop

The northwest corner of Montana is different from any other part of the state. It's wetter. The elevation is lower. It gets the most precipitation. Trees grow right up onto the mountaintops—if they haven't been cut.

Northwest Montana blends the Rocky Mountains with the Pacific Northwest. This overlap of ecosystems creates unique habitats. Western and mountain hemlocks, western redcedars, and grand firs grow in the wet areas, not far from forests of drought-tolerant lodgepoles, Douglas firs, and western larches. The valleys are narrow; the mountains are rounded from years of moist erosion; most summits reach only about 5,000 to 6,000 feet elevation.

Grizzly bears, wolves, mountain goats, moose, and even caribou live in the forests. The underbrush is thick with berries, shrubs, and ferns, and birdlife is abundant. Streams harbor rainbow, westslope cutthroat, bull and brook trout, and mountain whitefish.

Timber is the primary natural resource of this area. And timber is the primary point of conflict among residents of this area.

"There's no place like it anywhere in the state," stated Rick Bass. "It's real painful to live here and see it become like a tree farm, a monoculture of lodgepole pines infested with beetles. They've cut the forests of mixed conifers and replanted monocultures. You may as well spread honey on a rock and try to keep flies away as have one species and expect insects and plagues to stay away."

Bass is a writer from Yaak. He spoke about the frustrations of being an environmentalist who supports responsible logging. "Logging is a tough, noble, and admirable profession [when] done carefully and well," he said. "But the companies see higher revenues with clearcuts, and manipulate the timber workers against the environmentalists. They deflect the blame, and keep cutting."

Bass thinks that if the press and Forest Service would tell the truth, timber workers couldn't repress the knowledge that they're being jerked around by the mills. But he thinks the politicians have also played off it, and now the issue has become emotional and reason is left behind.

"If the mills were worker-owned, they'd support selective harvest. Selective, responsible harvest creates and prolongs their jobs. They'd be more responsible to the land they live on and raise families on."

Bass said he'll remain in Yaak as long as he can. "Till all the trees are gone, which may not be too long," he said somberly. "I'm not going to quit trying to get some country protected, but I'm not optimistic. I would welcome outside pressure to protect what's left of the Yaak, and stop terrible land use practices."

Pull into Yaak and look around to get a feel for this community. You'll see the Yaak Mercantile, and the Dirty Shame Saloon. And that's it. No homes, gardens, yards, school, playground, or other evidence of town.

"Yaak is really a strongly knit community, but not in the traditional sense," Bass explained. "That implicit sense of community comes from having the same reasons for being there. Nobody bothers each other. We have respect for each other and give each other lots of space. My nearest neighbors are a mile away. People there like the landscape, and nobody likes rules or authority, or bureaucracies, restrictions, and boundaries."

Just east of Yaak, Boyd Mill Cemetery provides another glimpse of the community. The cemetery is tucked into the forest under a canopy of tall trees. Gravestones show how people's identities here are tied to logging—instead of the usual angel or leaf motif, some of these folks are memorialized with a chainsaw pictured on the headstone.

The road from Yaak to Rexford winds through the forest and presents occasional views out to the surrounding clearcuts, to peaks of the Purcell Range and the fire lookout on Lost Horse Mountain, even as far east as the Whitefish Range.

Driving this road at sunset has a hypnotic effect. The sunlight coming low through the trees creates a dappled shadow and sun, almost like a strobe light. But shake off the spell and it's a great drive.

A few sections of the road traverse very steep mountainsides and have a lot of exposure with no guard rails. Combine this with the narrowness of the road and expect a few white-knuckle driving possibilities. If it weren't for the logging trucks barreling down the road at inappropriate speeds, it would be a perfect bicycling route.

We stayed at Webb Mountain Lookout for the night. For a nominal fee, the Forest Service rents selected cabins and fire lookouts for public use. The lookout shot straight up out of a pinnacle of rock just west of Lake Koocanusa.

We arrived at this eagle eyrie at dusk, in time to build a fire and watch daylight fade from the sky. Cloud fragments drifted around us; a massive rainstorm raged over the Ten Lakes Scenic Area to the north; it drizzled and cleared intermittently. The muted greens of forested slopes melded into the blues of distant ridges and peaks. The lights of Eureka clustered in a narrow valley to the northeast.

One side of the bridge over Lake Koocanusa disappeared into a dense cloud that hovered on the lake. People driving on the bridge must have had faith that the other end was connected to land, because you certainly couldn't see it. We watched headlights move slowly across, then vanish completely over the deep waters of the lake.

Sunrise the next morning came in pastel hues of pink and yellow. I bundled up against the considerable wind, and visited the outhouse. The only other outhouse view I've seen to rival this one was atop a volcano in Hawaii. While admiring the Purcell Range from this throne, I glanced up and noticed the guy wire anchoring the outhouse to a nearby tree. Another look revealed that the outhouse had a decided lean away from prevailing winds. That gave me pause to consider...

Outside, pockets of soil wedged into the bedrock summit held tiny gardens of wildflowers and grasses. Stonecrops and alumroots hugged the ground, avoiding the wind. The soft, hairy leaves of pussytoes held numerous drops of rainwater, like little rhinestones studding a green cashmere sweater. A cluster of tangerine-pink buckwheat buds were easing open, perhaps reluctant to expose the tender yellow petals to the blustery elements. Lupine and locoweed held firmly to the soil and leaned with each gust, swaying together to an irregular beat.

The wind blew away the cloud cover, and the lovely, muted view of last night solidified into a realistic look at what the logging industry is doing here. It isn't pretty.

Rexford used to be situated on the Kootenai River about two miles from its present location. When Libby Dam was built, residents opted to move the townsite rather than don scuba gear. There wasn't a whole lot to move anyway—Rexford had just a one-block business district. Many people left their clothes in the closets, secured the furniture, and watched their homes get picked up and plunked down on sites in the new Rexford.

Clara Fewkes came to this area in 1918 when her father got a job with a lumber company. That winter the whole family was down with the flu for six weeks—except 17-year-old Clara. She had eight patients in bed at the same time, the doctor came daily, and everyone recovered.

Fewkes went on to become a nurse, then quit to marry a patient and raise a family on the west side of the Kootenai River. They were "stump ranchers," meaning settlers who cut the trees and cleared the land to make room for crops and pasture.

"We were pretty isolated for a while there," she reminisced. "The currents in the river made the ice very treacherous, so when the ferry closed for the winter we stayed over there. I was the west-side midwife every winter.

"We had a wonderful social life. About every three or four

Northwest Montana blends the Rocky Mountains with the Pacific Northwest. This overlap of ecosystems creates unique habitats. Western and mountain hemlocks, western redcedars, and grand firs grow in the wet areas, not far from forests of drought-tolerant lodgepoles, Douglas firs, and western larches.

Above: *Successful angler.*
Top: *Old-growth western redcedar.*
Right: *Lake Koocanusa near Rexford.*

Facing page: *Yaak River Falls.*

weeks we'd hold a dance in a logger's empty bunkhouse. It cost fifty cents a couple, and we served a midnight lunch at the break.

"Nobody had any money, but we raised chickens and cows, and had a garden with everything you needed. We picked strawberries, gooseberries, currants, raspberries, and grew all kinds of vegetables. I canned vegetables and beef and venison, and rabbits, and chicken. My husband and I loved to fish. We did okay."

Fewkes loved the wildlife that lived in the adjacent forest. "The birds were so tame they'd eat off my hand," she said. "One chickadee brought her six young 'uns and lined them up and made them come eat off my fingers. The next day she started a new nest, so she had given them to me to finish raising while she started another batch.

"I also had a tame crow that learned to talk. He was a complete clown. He'd rap on the door with his beak and when I opened the door he'd drop his wings and bow and say, 'Hello, Mom.' Just like one of the kids. When the band of crows flew south they lit in the yard and talked at him all day but he just ignored them. They finally left, and he stayed around."

To ease the isolation a bit, the men on the west side strung telephone wire and connected about nineteen homes to the line. "We had big crank phones," Fewkes said. "We were just connected to each other, but that was fine. Why, we'd call the neighbors and see if they needed anything."

That spirit of supportiveness extended

beyond the west side too. Once a month the women met for their H.E.O. Club—Help Each Other. They sewed quilts and nips (bedroom slippers made of old mackinaws) for a veterans hospital, and filled Easter baskets for an orphanage.

When Fewkes was president of the H.E.O., she decided to have members relate memories of homesteading years at each meeting. "The first two came in with a regular pamphlet of stories written!" she exclaimed. "So then everyone else did. After a while we had a stack about a foot tall, so we took the best of it and in 1950 made a book."

Olga Johnson was the only person with a typewriter, so she edited *The Story of the Tobacco Plains Country*. The club members organized a Pioneer Club and had a picnic to raise funds to publish the book. "It was quite interesting," Fewkes laughed. "Some of those old-timers were ready to mix it over dates. One would say, 'So-and-so did this in 1892,' and another would say, 'No, it was 1894,' and we practically had to pull them apart."

Clara was widowed, and at age 72 married local storekeeper Bill Fewkes. They were avid rockhounds, and wintered in Arizona for 13 years. She especially liked photographing the bizarre cactus there.

At age 92, Fewkes is a sparkling, articulate, and elegant woman. Her home is warm and serene, and she now stays in Rexford year-round. Her library shelves are full of everything from children's stories to history, travel, rock-collecting, and silver-collecting. She makes quilts to benefit the local museum, knits and crochets, and volunteers at the historical village in Eureka. "Well, I get tired quicker than the younger folks," she admitted. "But I guess that's all right. I just take a nap, then get up and go again."

Eureka. The word is derived from the Greek word *heureka*, meaning "I have found." Those who have found home here apparently love it. Flower gardens adorn the neat homes, the main street businesses are housed in attractive Western-style false-fronts, the Tobacco River gurgles through town.

Tobacco Valley Historical Village sits next to the riverfront park. Visitors can tour the furnished log house, railroad depot, schoolhouse, library, caboose, and fire tower. A number of these buildings were moved here from the old Rexford townsite, including Bill Fewkes' general store. The store is now stocked with memorabilia and antiques. Sales of hand-made quilts and arts and crafts benefit the historical society. Ask around—you may find a quilt made by Clara.

Just south of Fortine, the backroads route turns off Highway 93 and goes south toward Trego. En route, stop to walk the easy, self-guided nature trail at Ant Flat. The name was derived exactly as you'd expect, from "all those gol' durned ant hills in the meadow." Ant Flat was the headquarters for the local ranger district from 1902 until 1963. Today, the buildings are used as a center to promote natural resource education.

In Trego, bear south on Route 36 and follow the signs reading "To Highway 37." This narrow asphalt road leads through countryside that brings to life the term "stumpfarming." Buildings sit out in fields of stumps; deer graze along the forest margins; sheds and trailers and houses are wedged into the clearings along Fortine Creek.

Sections of this route lull you into appreciating the beauty of moving slowly between steep slopes forested with tall conifers. Aspens line the streambanks, leaves fluttering at the slightest breeze. The underbrush is luxurious and green. Catch a flicker of movement as a white-tailed deer bounds out of sight; stop to savor some wild berries; listen to a hawk screaming as she circles her nest.

Just as you're certain all is well with the world, the route thrusts you into clearcut mania. Entire slopes are denuded, the straight lines of the logging boundaries out of place on the contours of the mountains. Logging roads slash across and through the naked slopes like a connect-the-dots game, but it doesn't make a pretty picture at the end.

This is the story everywhere you drive in the northwest

corner of Montana. Better drive this loop soon, because at this rate of logging there won't be any place left that hasn't been stripped and replanted in the same monotonous greens of one or two tree species.

Libby Dam has impounded the waters of the Kootenai River since 1975. The Kootenai originates in the Canadian Rockies and flows across the border to Montana. Lake Koocanusa was named by a Rexford woman, who combined three prominent geographic features to coin the name—*Koo*tenai River, *Can*ada, and the *USA*.

The dam serves as headwaters flood control for the Columbia River, generates electric power, and provides lake recreation opportunities. Fishing here has become legendary. A world record kamloops rainbow trout weighed in at 29.2 pounds. The 5-pound, 1.5-ounce Montana state record mountain whitefish caught here missed the world record by only half an ounce. Anglers fish for ling; kokanee salmon; sturgeon; and brook, cutthroat, rainbow, and bull trout. Boaters roar around on the lake, and assorted campgrounds are dotted up and down both sides of the lake. It's a very popular spot.

West of the dam, Libby serves as the Lincoln County seat. Over half of the employment in Lincoln County is timber-related, and the county is one of the country's major lumber producers. Libby Logger Days celebrates the heritage each summer with days of festivities, an arts and crafts fair, and friendly competitions. The Montana City Old Town Museum and Theatre, a recreated pioneer town with an opera house, is open from May through September.

Kootenai Falls west of Libby has a series of ledges and falls. It's about a half-mile walk from the highway to the river's edge, and there are broad ledges to sit on. We brought a picnic, then stretched out to relax and read in the sunshine.

The falls and the river canyon are revered by the Kootenai as a historic area for seeking visions, and for fish-ing. Proposals to dam the falls surface periodically, but have been beaten back each time. The region is in desperate need of employment opportunities, but dam construction provides only temporary employment. Environmental impact would be significant and permanent. The battle lines are drawn here, on the only waterfall left on a major river in the Pacific Northwest.

The highway runs along the river. A side trip south on Route 56 leads beneath the impressive Cabinet Mountains to Ross Creek Giant Cedars. An easy, self-guided trail leads through the grove of 500-year-old western red cedars. Some of these monoliths tower up to 175 feet, with trunks twelve feet in diameter. It's the kind of place where you whisper; where normal conversation is trite; where you can rekindle your spirit.

Route 508 between Highway 2 and Yaak meanders alongside the Yaak River, past lovely Yaak Falls, and through tiny settlements. One-lane bridges stretched across feeder creeks to homesites; slash piles were stacked around the perimeters of newly-cut fields of stumps; the condition of the houses and shacks demonstrated the poor economic conditions here. It is a tough place to make a living.

As I drove through the drizzle, I realized there was one business venture that would be a sure success here. Tarps. Making durable, waterproof tarps. Everywhere you looked, bright blue, hunter green, and shouting orange tarps sprouted. There were even more tarps than satellite dishes, and that's a considerable number to beat.

Tarps covered the woodpiles, the shed roofs, the lean-tos, the entryways, the barbecue pits, the trailers, and the doghouses. Shredded pieces of tarps flapped in the breeze, pieces of torn tarps blew across the road, brand new tarps imprisoned beneath snug ropes strained to break loose. An entrepreneur would have a guaranteed clientele and could advertise the quality of the product as tested under the rigorous conditions in northwest Montana, here in the land o' tarps and stumps.

Lake Koocanusa was named by a Rexford woman, who combined three prominent geographic features to coin the name—*Koo*tenai River, *Can*ada, and the *USA*.

Red rock formation along Rock Creek, Sapphire Mountains.

I N D E X